The Sabbath

and

The Lord's Day

By

H. M. Riggle

Life Assurance Ministries
PO Box 11587
Glendale, Arizona 85318

The Sabbath and The Lord's Day

By H. M. Riggle

Printed in the United States of America

Life Assurance Ministries
PO Box 11587
Glendale, Arizona 85318

623-572-9549 (information)
800-355-7073 (orders only)
623-572-3035 (fax)
Email: dale@ratzlaf.com
Web Site: www.LifeAssuranceMinistries.com

ISBN 0-9627546-7-6

Preface

Before the death of the first apostles of Christ certain law-teachers troubled the churches, trying to impose upon them the rites of Moses' law. In a large assembly of apostles and elders at Jerusalem, it was fully decided and settled not to bind the law upon Gentile Christians (see Acts 15). In the Epistles of Paul powerful arguments are brought forth to teach the abrogation of the law and the superior qualities of the gospel, the law of Christ. The apostle declares the law-teachers "pervert the gospel of Christ," are "vain janglers," "understanding neither what they say, nor whereof they affirm."

After the death of the apostles a number of sects arose that taught the law is binding and enjoined the observance of the Jewish Sabbath. Among these were the Ebionites, who flourished in the second century and dissented from the general church. They were among the rankest heretics of their time.

About the time of the Reformation a body of people arose in England that zealously advocated the observance of the seventh day. They had many able ministers and writers, and published many books. Today their work has become entirely extinct.

A small body of people known as Seventh-day Baptists arose in 1664. They are now very few in number.

In 1846 Seventh-day Adventists began teaching the Jewish Sabbath. They have been very zealous. They have poured out their means by the millions and have filled the land with their literature. Probably no other small body of people on earth have published and circulated as much literature over the world as these. No other people have met with more disappointments during their existence. Miller, the founder of the Adventist movement finally opposed the Sabbath, and warned his followers against its observance. Scores of their most prominent ministers have at different times renounced the faith as an error. Many have been led into infidelity as a result of the mistakes of Adventism. We believe the whole system is a yoke of bondage.

These law-teachers travel from hamlet to city, scattering their doctrines by lecturing in tents and halls and by distributing tracts, papers, and books among the people. Although but few accept the doctrine, hundreds become unsettled, and can scarcely be reached by the truth. To counteract this influence and to set forth the truth, is the object of this book. It will be found to be pointed and thorough on the subject. It is a complete treatise on all the important points relating to the Sabbath and the Lord's Day.

Having received a written permission from D. M. Canright, of Grand Rapids, Mich., I have made some choice quotations from his excellent work *Seventh-Day Adventism Renounced.* Mr. Canright was for a number of years a very prominent minister and writer of the Adventist faith. At the time he renounced their doctrines in 1887, he held a number of the highest offices in the society, and was, no doubt, one of the ablest ministers they have ever had. Hear his testimony:

"After keeping the seventh day and extensively advocating it for over a quarter of a century, I became satisfied that it was an error, and that the blessing of God did not go with the keeping of it. Like thousands of others, when I embraced the seventh-day Sabbath I thought that the argument was all on one side, so plain that one hour's reading ought to settle it, so clear that no man could reject the Sabbath and be honest. The only marvel to me was that everybody did not see and embrace it.

"But after keeping it twenty-eight years; after having persuaded more than a thousand others to keep it; after having read my Bible through, verse by verse, more than twenty times; after having scrutinized, to the very best of my ability every text, line, and word in the Bible having the remotest bearing upon the Sabbath question; after having looked up all these, both in the original and in many translations; after having searched in lexicons, concordances, commentaries, and dictionaries; after having read armfuls of books on both sides of the question; after having read every line in all the early church Fathers upon this point; and having written several works in favor of the seventh day, which were satisfactory to my brethren; after having debated the question for more than a dozen times; after seeing the fruits of keeping it, and weighing all the evidence in the fear of God, I am fully settled in my own mind and convinced that the evidence is against the keeping of the seventh day."—*Seventh-day Adventism Renounced,* pages 185, 186.

Such testimony is of great value and weight. In the chapters "The Sabbath on a Round Earth," and "The Law," I quote from his work at some length. Also, scattered throughout the book are a few quotations from D. S. Warner's former book on *The Sabbath.* In some cases I have given extracts of the quotations, instead of giving them in full or verbatim. I ask the reader to give this book a careful study with unbiased mind; and I believe the truth contained in its pages will be flashlights from the throne of God to your understanding.

Yours in Christian love,—H. M. Riggle

Introduction to the Revised Edition

If a system of worship is wrong, then all the labor to build up a system is misdirected effort. We sincerely believe that the whole Sabbatarian contention is resting upon a wrong premise. After a most careful study of the question, we believe that the Scriptures do not support the observance of the seventh day under the Christian dispensation.

All truth runs parallel. Truth never contradicts. If we can adduce a single truth against the observance of Saturday-keeping under the gospel, then let it be borne in mind that every other truth is against it. If we can sustain our position by a single truth, then all truth upholds it. On this eternal principle we build our arguments. It is the truth we want. With open hearts let us carefully investigate the whole subject.

I kindly ask our Sabbatarian friends to go with me in the perusal of this important subject, and in our study together, may the Holy Spirit lead us into a correct knowledge of the truth.

—H. M. Riggle

Contents

Contents Continued

Contents Continued

The Sabbath: When Originated And When First Enjoined Upon Man

The plan of redemption was conceived in the mind of God prior to the foundation of the world. It was a mystery then hid in him alone. Long ages before that mystery was unlocked to mankind in the person of Jesus Christ, who made the world's atonement, it cast a love-betokening shadow upon earth. That shadow was the law. The law embraced the five books of Moses—Genesis, Exodus, Leviticus, Numbers, and Deuteronomy. In proof of this, I cite a quotation from each book.

Paul says that women "are commanded to be under obedience, as also saith the law" (1 Cor. 14:34). Where does the law say this? In Gen. 3:16. I quote from the LXX: "The submission shall be to thy husband, and he shall rule over thee." Genesis, then, is in the law. "The law had said, Thou shalt not covet" (Rom. 7:7). Where? In Exod. 20:17. So Exodus is in the law. Jesus makes two quotations from the law: 1. "Thou shalt love the Lord thy God with all thy heart." This is taken from Deut. 6:5. 2. "Thou shalt love thy neighbor as thyself." This is from Lev. 19:18. So both Deuteronomy and Leviticus are a part of the law. Again: "Have ye not read in the law, how that on the Sabbath days the priests in the temple profane the Sabbath, and are blameless?" (Matt. 12:5). This is from Num. 28:9. So all the five books of Moses are embraced in "the law."

"The law having a shadow of good things to come" (Heb. 10:1). The whole law system was but a shadow, containing types and figures of the plan of perfect redemption. Its passover, atonements, sacrifices, offerings, tabernacle, temple, altars, blood, priests, circumcision, and sabbaths, all belonged to the law of shadows going before.

Among the promises of coming redemption was that of Shiloh—the rest-giver (Gen. 49:10). "And his rest shall be glorious" (Isa. 11:10). In fulfillment, Jesus came, saying, "Come unto me…and I will give you rest. And ye shall find rest unto your souls" (Matt. 11:28, 29). In the law of shadows there must be a type of this sweet and tranquil rest found in redeeming grace. Hence God set apart one day in seven, the seventh, as a "sabbath of rest."

"Sabbath" means "rest." Rest is the sole idea of the term. The law said, "Six days may work be done; but in the seventh is the Sabbath of rest" (Exod. 31:15). This is made still clearer in the Septuagint, where it is rendered, "But the seventh day is the Sabbath, a holy rest to the Lord." That sabbath, or rest, was "a shadow of things to come." It reached its fulfillment in Christ, in whom our souls have found an everlasting rest (see Col. 2:14-17; Heb. 4:1-11).

The Sabbath, then, was instituted by God, among the types and shadows of his great redemption. It pointed back to the creation, and forward to Christ, just as the Passover pointed back to Israel's exodus from Egyptian bondage and forward to "Christ our passover, sacrificed for us." Whether, therefore, the Sabbath was instituted before Moses or not, it belonged to the law of types and shadows. Sacrifices began in the family of Adam, circumcision began with Abraham, yet both were nailed to the cross with all the ordinances of Moses.

But let us investigate, and find just when and where the Sabbath was first enjoined upon man. Saturday-keepers lay no small stress upon a supposed pre-Mosaic Sabbath. In fact, it is one of their main pillars. Back there in the dim past the events of an age were covered by a few lines in the Bible. Yet "the main reliance of Sabbatarians is upon arguments drawn from those remote times of darkness, while in the New Testament they find little to support their theories, but much to explain away."

The scholarship of the world is somewhat divided on the subject of a pre-Mosaic Sabbath. Much has been written on both sides of the question. In either case it has little bearing on present observance. But since our Sabbatarian friends rely greatly upon a belief in Sabbath-observance from Eden, I desire to set before the reader what I sincerely believe to be the truth of the matter. After reading much on both sides of the controversy, I have been led into the settled conviction that the argument for Sabbath-observance from Eden down through the Patriarchal age rests upon a very sandy foundation. I shall submit the following proofs against it:

There is not one command in the book of Genesis to keep the seventh day as a Sabbath. In the language of Canright, "There is no statement that any of the patriarchs kept the Sabbath or knew anything about it. Sabbatarians say the record is so brief that it was omitted. Their proof, then, is *what was left out!*"

The first mention of the Sabbath as a rest-day enjoined upon man that is recorded in the Bible is found in Exod. 16:23-30. This was twenty-five hundred years after the creation of man. It was a new command to the Jews. On Friday, Moses said to the people, "Tomorrow is a solemn rest, a holy Sabbath unto the Lord" (verse 23, *Revised Version).* On Saturday, he said, "Today is a Sabbath unto the Lord" (verse 25). "So the people rested on the seventh day" (verse 30). "And the people keep Sabbath on the seventh day" (LXX). This language, with its context, seems to prove that the children of Israel *there* and *then* began *resting* on the seventh day; that the keeping of the Sabbath was a new thing to them. Their deliverance from Egypt marked a new era in their history. At this time the Lord gave them a new year and a new beginning of months. (See Exod. 12:2.) So, also, he for the first time gave them the Sabbath (Exodus 16). Many scriptures teach this fact, a few of which are given below.

"Wherefore I caused them to go forth out of the land of Egypt, and brought them into the wilderness. Moreover also I gave them my sabbaths, to be a sign between me and them" (Ezek. 20:10, 12). This text is conclusive. It simply states that God *gave them* the Sabbath when he brought them out of Egypt. "I gave them my sabbaths" implies the act of committing it to them, and proves that they did not have it before. It was a new thing to them, and only for them. The place where God gave Israel the Sabbath was "the wilderness." It was given as a sign between himself and that nation. So positively teaches the text quoted.

"And remember that thou wast a servant in the land of Egypt, and that the Lord thy God brought thee out thence through a mighty hand, and by a stretched out arm:

THEREFORE the Lord thy God *commanded thee to keep the Sabbath Day"* (Deut. 5:15). God commanded Israel to keep the Sabbath as a memorial of their deliverance from Egypt. Then, they never kept it until the reason existed for keeping it. Thus, it was first enjoined upon them in the wilderness.

The covenant enjoining the seventh day was not made before Moses. "The Lord our God made a covenant with us in Horeb. The Lord made not this covenant with our fathers, but with us, even us, who are all of us here alive this day" (Deut. 5:2, 3). "Then follows a recital of the Ten Commandments, the covenant referred to. So if we are to credit the inspired statement of Moses, we must admit that the law embodying the seventh-day Sabbath had never been given to the ancestors of the Jewish nation. Nay, "The Lord made not this covenant with out fathers, but with us, even us, who are all of us here alive this day."

We affirm that every assumption that the Sabbath had been previously given is a direct contradiction of these texts.

"Thou camest down also upon Mount Sinai, and spakest with them from heaven…and *makest known* unto them thy holy Sabbath" (Neh. 9:13, 14). "Though the Sabbath had been introduced a short time before when the manna first fell, it is but natural that Nehemiah should speak of it with the rest of the law, as given on Sinai, by the audible voice of God, . . . and made a statute in Israel. If, then, we credit the testimony of Nehemiah, we trace the origin of that Sabbath to Moses in the wilderness. There is where God came down and gave that law."

I shall now quote from *The Sabbath* and also from Canright. "Smith and Barnum's *Dictionary of the Bible* says, 'In Exod. 16:23-29 we find the first incontrovertible institution of the day, as one given to, and to be kept by, the children of Israel. Shortly afterward it was re-enacted in the fourth commandment.'

"'There is no express mention of it previous to the time of *Moses.'—Jahn's Biblical Archaeology.*

"'The celebration of the seventh day as a day consecrated to Jehovah, is first mentioned after the Exodus from Egypt, and seems to have preceded the Sinaitic legislation, which merely confirmed and invested it with the highest authority. There is no trace of its celebration in the patriarchal times.'—Chambers' *Encyclopedia.*

"'The first record of its observance by the Jews is mentioned in Exod. 16:25, when, in addition to its being observed in remembrance of the original rest-day of the creation, it was celebrated also in memento of the day of freedom of the Jews from Egyptian *bondage.'—People's Cyclopedia.*

"Smith's Bible Dictionary says of the argument on Gen. 2:1-3 for the institution of the Sabbath in Eden, 'The whole argument is very precarious....There is no record of its celebration in patriarchal times.'

"'The early Christian writers are generally...silent on the subject of a primitive Sabbath....Such examination as we have been able to institute, has disclosed no belief in its existence, while some indications are found of a notion that the Sabbath began with *Moses.'—Kitto.*

"Justin Martyr, who wrote only forty-four years after the death of John, and who was well acquainted with the doctrines of the apostles, denied that the Sabbath originated at creation. Thus after naming Adam, Abel, Enoch, Lot, and Melchizedek, he says: 'Moreover, all those righteous men already mentioned, though they kept no Sabbaths, were pleasing to God.'—*Dialog with Trypho,* chap. 19.

"'Enoch and all the rest, who neither were circumcised after the flesh, nor observed Sabbaths, nor any other rites, seeing that Moses enjoined such observances.

"'For if there was no need of circumcision before Abraham, or of the observance of the Sabbaths,...before Moses, no more need is here of them now.

"'As, then, circumcision began with Abraham, and the Sabbath...with Moses, and it has been proved they were enjoined on account of the hardness of your people's hearts, so it was necessary, in accordance with the Father's will, that they should have an end in him, who was born of a virgin, of the family of Abraham.' —*Justin Martyr to Trypho, a Jew."* Thus it will be seen that Justin Martyr understood that the Sabbath began wih Moses, and ended in Christ. This is in perfect harmony with the Scriptural teaching.

"Irenaeus says: 'Abraham believed God without circumcision and the Sabbath.'—*Adv. Hoeres,* Lib. IV, ch. 30.

"Tertullian, A.D. 200, said: 'Let them show me that Adam Sabbatized, or that Abel in presenting his holy offerings to God pleased him by Sabbath observance, or that Enoch who was translated was an observer of the *Sabbath.'—Against the Jews,* sec. IV."

Eusebius, A.D. 324, the father of church history, says:
"They [the patriarchs] did not, therefore, regard circumcision, nor observe the Sabbath, neither do we....Such things as these do not belong to Christians." Book I, ch. 4.

Here, then, we have the testimony from the historical records from the second and third centuries that the Sabbath was not enjoined upon, nor observed by, the people of God till Moses' time, or for 2,500 years after creation. The early church did not believe that the Sabbath originated at creation. I shall add the testimony of eminent men.

"The transactions in the wilderness above recited were the first actual institution of the Sabbath." — Paley:
Watson's Institutes, vol. II, p. 515.
"The Sabbath is no where mentioned, or even obscurely alluded to, either in the general history of the world before the call of Abraham, or in that of the first three Jewish patriarchs."—Paley: *Wakefield's Theology.*

"Whether its institution was ever made known to Adam, or whether any commandment relative to its observance was given previous to the delivery of the law on Mt. Sinai...cannot be ascertained."—John Milton: *Christian Doctrine,* vol. I, p. 299.

"That the Israelites had not so much as heard of the Sabbath before this time [the wilderness], seems to be confirmed by several passages of the prophets." —*John Milton.*

"Now as to the imposing of the seventh-day Sabbath upon men from Adam to Moses, of that we find nothing in holy writ, either from precept or example."—John Bunyan: *Complete Works,* page 892. On page 895 of the same book Bunyan says, "The seventh-day Sabbath, therefore, was not from paradise, nor from nature, nor from the fathers, but from the wilderness and from Sinai." Bunyan was well versed In Scripture.

From all the foregoing it is clearly seen that the united scriptural testimony, the most authentic historical records, the teachings of the most highly learned and eminent men, all point to the wilderness and Sinai for the institution of the Sabbath. It is clearly traced to Moses and the law. Upon what, then, do Saturday-keepers base their claim for a pre-Mosaic Sabbath? Upon their own misinterpretation of the words of Moses in Gen. 2:2, 3. They argue that God rested, blessed, and sanctified the seventh day in Eden, and that hence an obligation rests upon all to observe it.

That this reasoning is incorrect and the whole argument unsound I shall now proceed to show.

1. The Book of Genesis, including these words, was not written at the time of the creation of man, but twenty-five hundred years later, by Moses himself. In fact, this statement of Moses' in Gen. 2:2, 3 was not written until after the covenant enjoining the seventh-day Sabbath upon the Jews had been delivered upon Sinai.

2. The language clearly proves that God did not bless and sanctify the day back at Eden when he rested, but at a later date. "And he rested on the seventh day from all his work which he had made. And God blessed the seventh day, and sanctified it: because that *in it He had rested* from all his work which God created and made." He blessed and sanctified the day *"because* in it HE HAD rested." He rested back in Eden. But God's rest did not make the day holy. It was not holy in itself. Twenty-five hundred years later God in the wilderness blessed and sanctified the seventh day as a holy day to the Jewish nation, and assigned as one reason for doing so that "In it he had rested." After God blessed and sanctified the day in the wilderness, Moses wrote the book of Genesis; and in writing the account of the creation he

said that God began resting on the seventh day from all his work, and that the same day on which God had rested he now sanctified and blessed. Here again the inspired Word points to the wilderness for the institution of the Sabbath.

"As this narrative, i.e., Gen. 2:2, 3, was composed after the delivery of the law, for their special instruction, so this passage was only intended to confirm more forcibly that institution; or that it is to be understood as If Moses had said, 'God rested on the seventh day, which he has since blessed and sanctified.' "— Kitto's Cyclopedia of Biblical Literature. To this we say amen. The language of Genesis II cannot be understood in any other light, unless the text is wrested.

"As the seventh day was erected into a Sabbath, on account of God's resting upon that day from the work of creation, it was but natural enough in the historian, when he had related the history of the creation, and of God's ceasing from it on the seventh day, to add, 'And God blessed the seventh day, and sanctified it, because that on it he had rested from all his work which God created and made'; although the blessing and sanctification, that is, the religious distinction and appropriation of that day, were not made till many ages after. The words do not assert that God then blessed and sanctified the seventh day, but that he blessed and sanctified it *for that reason.*" Paley: *Moral and Political Philosophy,* Book IV, ch. 7.

On this point I quote the following from Canright:

"As Moses wrote his books after he came to Sinai, after the Sabbath had been given in the wilderness, he here mentions one reason why God thus gave them the seventh day, viz.: because God himself had set the example at creation; had worked six days and rested the seventh. Such use of language is common. We say General Grant was born at such a time. We do not mean that he was a general then, but we mention it by anticipation, using a title which he afterwards bore. So in Gen. 3:20, 'Adam called his wife's name Eve, because she was the mother of all living.' Here is a future fact stated as though it had already occurred. So 1 Sam. 4:1, the Jews 'pitched beside Eben-ezer.'

But the place was not named Eben-ezer till years after (1 Sam. 7:12). 'Judas Iscariot, which also was the traitor' (Luke 6:16). Here a future fact with regard to Judas is mentioned when he is first spoken of, though the act of betrayal did not take place till years later. Just so when the seventh day is first mentioned, its sanctification is referred to, though it did not occur till afterwards."

3. "Though the record from Adam to Moses covers a period of twenty-five hundred years; though we appear to have a full account of the religious customs and worship of the patriarchs, such as Noah, Abraham, Isaac, Jacob, Joseph, etc., though we are told about circumcision, the altar, the sacrifices, the priests, the tithe, the oath, marriage, feast-days, etc.; yet never a word is said about anyone keeping the Sabbath."— *Canright.*

The first mention of the Sabbath's being kept by anyone is recorded in Exodus 16. It began with Moses and was instituted in the wilderness. To go back of Moses for proof in favor of Saturday-keeping is going outside the Bible, into the fogs and mists of speculation and darkness.

The Sabbath a Jewish Institution

Law-teachers try in every way possible to evade the fact that the Sabbath was only Jewish. To admit this would prove that they are trying to revive an abolished institution which belonged wholly to a single nation in a former dispensation. But this is the truth set forth in the plainest terms.

Says God, "I gave *them* [the Jews] my sabbaths, to be a sign between me and *them*" (Ezek. 20:12). Not to angels in heaven and to Gentile nations on earth, but to the Jews, God gave the Sabbath. If I gave John a dollar, is it not John's dollar? "I gave them [the Jews] my Sabbath," saith the Lord. Is it not their Sabbath? Notice how plain the record is that God gave the Sabbath to the Jews, and to no others. "The Lord hath given you the Sabbath" (Exod. 16:29). "Speak thou also unto the *children of Israel,* saying, Verily, my sabbaths ye shall keep" (Exod.

31:13.) "It is a sign between me and the children of Israel" (vs. 17). "The *children of Israel* shall keep the Sabbath...through THEIR generations" (vs. 16).

Surely this is plain. But right in the face of such positive declarations, Sabbatarians contend that the decalog enjoining the observance of the seventh day rules the universe of God; hence is binding upon angels in heaven and upon all nations of earth. Therefore they argue that the angels keep the seventh-day Sabbath. Let us examine it.

"The Lord our God made a covenant with us in Horeb. The Lord made not this covenant with our fathers, but with us, even us, who are all of us here alive this day. The Lord talked with you face to face in the mount out of the midst of the fire,... saying, I am the Lord thy God, which brought thee out of the land of Egypt, from the house of bondage....Keep the Sabbath Day to sanctify it, as the Lord thy God hath commanded thee. Six days thou shalt labor, and do all thy work: but the seventh day is the Sabbath of the Lord thy God: in it thou shalt not do any work, thou, nor thy son, nor thy daughter, nor thy man servant, nor thy maid servant, nor thine ox, nor thine ass, nor any of thy cattle, nor thy stranger that is within thy gates;...And remember that thou wast a servant in the land of Egypt, and that the Lord thy God brought thee out thence through a mighty hand and by a stretched out arm: *therefore* the Lord thy God commanded *thee* to keep the Sabbath." "These words the Lord spake unto all your assembly....And he wrote them in two tables of stone" (Deut. 5:2-15, 22).

This is the Sabbath commandment as enjoined in the decalog. Saturday-keepers contend that this command is obligatory upon all nations and even upon angels in heaven; but a careful reading of the foregoing will show that it was given only to the Jews, to the children of Israel. It was but a Jewish institution. This covenant enjoining the seventh-day Sabbath Moses declares was not made with their fathers (the patriarchs), nor with Gentiles, nor with angels in heaven, "but with us, *even us,* who are all of us here alive this day."

It was made with the children of Israel only. It applied only to them. "I am the Lord thy God, which brought thee out of the land of Egypt, from the house of bondage." Were the angels in Egyptian bondage? Would not that sound a little queer to Gabriel and the heavenly host? Were the Gentile nations there? How does this apply to us Americans? Were we in Egypt? Not many of us. We are free-born. Then, to whom are the words applicable? The answer is obvious: To the Jewish nation, and to no others. Notice the language: "Keep the Sabbath Day....The seventh is the Sabbath. Remember that thou wast a servant in the land of Egypt, and that the Lord thy God brought thee out... *therefore* [or for that reason] the Lord thy God commanded thee to keep the Sabbath Day." Language could not be framed to teach more clearly that the Sabbath commandment was to the Jews only. So it read on the tables of stone, and when law teachers apply such language to Gentile nations, or to angels in heaven, they prove that they "understand neither what they say, nor whereof they affirm" (1 Tim. 1:7).

"Take the Sabbath commandment: 'Thy son, nor thy daughter, thy man servant, nor thy maid servant, nor thy cattle, nor thy stranger that is within thy gates' (Exod. 20:10). Think of that commandment being given to angels in heaven! 'Sons,' 'daughters,' and 'thy neighbor's wife' (vs. 17), when they neither marry nor are given in marriage. Again: 'Cattle,' 'ox' 'ass,' etc. Do the angels own cattle and work oxen and asses in heaven? So 'man servants and maid servants.' This means bond-servants or slaves, such as the Hebrews owned in those days...*Their* 'man servants and maid servants' (Exod. 20:17). But do the angels own slaves? Did Adam have servants in Eden? Do Christians now have slaves? Will the redeemed own them hereafter? What nonsense to apply this law to the angels and to Eden and to heaven! This word was specially adapted to the social condition of the Jews as a nation in the land of Canaan, and to no others.

"Once more: 'Thy stranger that is within thy gates' (vs. 10). As everybody knows, 'the stranger' was the Gentile. 'Within thy gates' was a common expression meaning within your cities or dwelling in your land. It has no reference to living on your farm or inside the gates that enclose your farm, as Adventists always explain it. The towns were walled in and entered by gates. Here is where the judges sat and business was done. Thus: 'All that went in at the gate of his city' (Gen. 23:10). 'Judges and officers shalt thou make thee in all thy gates' (Deut. 16:18). To this custom of the Jews the Sabbath commandment refers. All the Gentiles dwelling in their cities among them must be made to keep the Sabbath. This shows it to be a national law, worded in all its parts to fit the circumstances of the Jews at that time.

"This command, then, could not apply to any but the Jews."—*Canright.*

"The laws regulating how the Sabbath should be kept show that it was a local institution adapted only to the Jewish workshop and to that warm climate." "All the rigorous limitations and exactions of the Sabbath Day, as under the Jewish law, could only be carried out by a small people in a limited territory where the church bore rule. A particular day, the seventh (Deut. 5:12, 13); definite hours, sunset to sunset (Lev. 23:32); no fires must be built on the Sabbath (Exod. 35:3); they must neither bake nor boil that day (Exod. 16:23); they must not go out of the house (Exod. 16:29); they were stoned to death for picking up a stick (Num. 15:32). Their priests must offer two lambs that day (Num. 28:9); they must compel all among them, living in their land, to keep it (Exod. 20:10). It was to be wholly a day of rest." —*Canright.*

Such was the Jewish law. We are not Jews, nor under the Jewish law. "What things soever the law saith, it saith to them who are under the law" (Rom. 3:19). But the Gentiles "have not the law" (Rom. 2:14); and Christians "are not under the law, but under grace" (Rom. 6:14).

That Jewish law could not be universal. In cold countries people would freeze without fires, and suffer without warm food. Adventists with all their blind zeal cannot keep the day according to the law. "They go many miles on the Sabbath and drive; they offer no lambs; they can compel no one to keep it; nor do they stone those who break it." In this they expose their folly in trying to observe an obsolete Jewish day.

In Hos. 2:11 the Sabbath is plainly said to be "her Sabbaths that is, Israel's sabbaths. It is classed in with Jewish "feasts" and "new moons," and all belonged to "her"—Israel. This settled the matter. The seventh-day Sabbath is the Jewish Sabbath. To this day the Jews claim the Sabbath as their institution.

The Jewish Sabbath Ceremonial in Nature

"Ceremony. Outward rite; external form in religion."—*Webster.* "An outward form or rite in religion; anything or observance held *sacred.*"—*International Encyclopedic Dictionary.* This is exactly what the observance of the Sabbath was in Jewish worship. The day in itself was not holy. One twenty-four hours of time is no better than another, unless *made so.* In the nature of days there is no difference; there is nothing in one that makes it differ from another. All nature continues the same. Then, the only way in which one day can become holy is by divine appointment.

Moral obligations are not made, or do not become so by mere appointment. They exist in their very nature. Murder, idolatry, blasphemy, stealing, adultery, etc., are morally wrong. Had God given no special command against these things, they would have been wrong in their nature. But it would never have been wrong to work on the seventh day unless God had given a commandment to rest in it. The day in itself was not holy, any more than the other days. God made it holy. He "sanctified it" (Gen. 2:3); he "hallowed it" (Exod. 20:11). This act of the Lord made the day holy. But did it make it holy for all time and eternity? I mean this: Did God's appointment, his sanctification of that particular day, set it apart as being holy forever? If so, then every other day and thing made holy by God's appointment would remain so forever.

Other days were made just as holy as the seventh day. In Leviticus 23 are the feasts of the Lord, which were all "holy convocations." These were the ceremonial seasons. The first of these feasts on the list is the weekly seventh-day Sabbath. Verses 1-3. It is spoken of as a "rest, an holy convocation; ye shall do no work therein." Next comes the Lord's Passover. Verses 5-8: "In the first day ye shall have an holy convocation: ye shall do no servile work therein." Next the feast of harvest (vss. 10-14). After this the feast of Pentecost (vss. 15-21). It also was "a holy convocation," and the Jews were forbidden to work on that day (vs. 21). In fact, a careful reading of the entire chapter shows that all those special feast-days were holy days. They were made so by God's appointment.

The Day of Atonement was just as holy as the weekly Sabbath. "There shall be a Day of Atonement: it shall be an holy convocation unto you;…and whatsoever soul it be that doeth any work in that same day, the same soul will I destroy from among his people. Ye shall do no manner of work:…It shall be unto you a Sabbath of rest" (vss. 27-32).

The Day of Atonement, was a holy sabbath day—so holy that it was death to work on it; yet all those holy days have ceased to be such, and are now common working-days. Adventists admit that those holy days—made so by God's appointment—were ceremonial and nailed to the cross. They do not attempt to keep them. But the seventh day was exactly like these—made holy by God's appointment. Hence it was ceremonial, and was nailed to the cross. I quote from Canright:

"So, then, holiness can be put upon a day, taken from it, or changed to another day. It is not necessarily a permanent, unchangeable affair. Let Sabbatarians meditate here awhile. More still: A day once appointed, and made a holy sabbath-day by God himself, may cease to be such and become even hateful to God. Thus: Isa. 1:13, 14, 'The new moons and sabbaths, the calling of the assemblies, I cannot away with; it is *iniquity,* even the solemn meeting. Your new moons and your appointed feasts my soul hateth: they are a trouble unto me; I am weary to bear them.' All these holy days God himself had appointed. Is it any proof, then, that a particular day is holy now because it was once holy? None whatever.

"Notice also how many other things were made holy by God's appointment. Under the *law* we read of 'the holy temple,' 'the holy hill,' 'the holy ark,' 'the holy instruments,' 'the holy vessels,' 'the holy water,' 'the holy perfume,' 'the holy altar,' 'the holy veil,' 'the holy linen coat,' 'the holy ointment,' 'the holy nation,' 'the holy Sabbath,' etc. Those pertained to the worship and service of God In his *holy temple* [tabernacle], which was 'only a shadow,' 'figure,' or 'type of the *true* temple'—the 'spiritual house' of Christ, 'his body, the church.' While they stood as *types* they were 'holy,' and no longer. They had no inherent holiness, but were made holy by the command of God. (*Law and Gospel,* p. 43, by S. C. Adam.)

"Like all these holy things, the seventh day had no holiness in itself. It had to be 'made' so (Mark 2:27). The sanctity of the day did not rest upon the nature of the day itself, but, like a hundred other hallowed things, simply upon God's appointment, which may be altered any time at his will."

No man could murder, blaspheme, commit adultery, steal, etc., for years and be a Christian. Why? Because these things are morally wrong. But the most zealous Saturday-keepers admit that such men as Luther, Wesley, Bunyan, and thousands of others, who never kept the seventh day (some of whom wrote against its observance), were highly eminent Christian men. Adventists' literature says so. They readily admit that there are many Christians who do not keep Saturday. How is this? A moment's reflection here ought to convince them that the keeping of the Sabbath as enjoined in the law was ceremonial in its nature.

The Sabbath on a Round Earth[1]

In their very nature all purely moral laws are universal and eternal in their application, are binding in heaven, in Eden, on Jews or Gentiles, saints or sinners, now or hereafter. Test the particular seventh day, Saturday, by that rule, and it fails everywhere. All the universe might keep a seventh part of time, but not the same seventh part. Not knowing this, see what blunder Mrs. White made. She says: "I saw that the Sabbath would never be done away, but the redeemed saints, *and* all *the angelic host,* will observe it in honor of the great Creator, to all *eternity.*"—*Spiritual Gifts,* vol 1., p. 113. Uriah Smith, a leading Adventist, says: "We infer that the higher orders of his intelligences keep the Sabbath also....The Sabbath of each of his creatures will be the Sabbath of all the rest, so that all will observe *the same period together* for the same *purpose.*"— *Biblical Institute,* page 145. In a discussion held at Oakland, Pa., I publicly asked leading ministers of the Adventist movement whether it is their teaching that God and the angels of heaven keep the seventh day with them. I asked in particular: "Do you believe that when the sun sets on Friday evening and you begin keeping Sabbath, that God and the angels begin also to keep the same time, and thus the heavenly hosts and you folks on earth keep the same identical time together?" They both replied: *"This is our teaching."*

Look at the utter absurdity and impossibility of the theory. All intelligent beings in heaven and earth and on all the planets, keep "the same period together." Adventists, like the Jews, keep Sabbath from sunset to sunset (Lev. 23:32). Now I shall prove by stubborn facts that they cannot all "observe the same period together."

Everybody knows that it is Saturday in India some twelve

---

[1] Much of the substance of this chapter is selected from *Seventh-day Adventism Renounced,* by Canright.

hours sooner than it is here, and that it is Saturday here twelve hours after it has ceased to be Saturday there. In Australia the day begins eighteen hours sooner than it does in California. So the seventh-day brethren in California are working nearly the whole time that their brethren in Australia are keeping Sabbath! Come even nearer home than that. The sun sets about three hours later in California than it does in Maine. So when the Seventh-day Adventists in Maine begin to keep the Sabbath at sunset Friday evening their own brethren in California, where the sun is yet three hours high, will still be at work for three hours! So very few of them on this earth "observe the same period together." While some of them are keeping Sabbath on one part of the earth, others of them are at work on another part of the earth. How much less, then, do all the heavenly host keep the same period with men on earth.

Now, if, as Mrs. White and Uriah Smith say, the angels keep our Sabbath, the question is, With which party do they keep it? With those in Australia, or those in America? If the angels keep the Sabbath at the same time the Sabbatarians keep it in Australia, then the Sabbatarians in America are working while the angels keep Sabbath, and so, of course, the angels work while those here rest. So we see how absolutely false and absurd is the theory that all can keep the Sabbath at the same time.

Adventists at Washington, D. C., really suppose that when the sun sets Friday evening and they begin keeping Sabbath, the Lord and the angels begin keeping it, too. Oh, what blindness! If the Lord keeps the Sabbath with them at Washington, then he does not keep it with their brethren on the other side of the globe, because they begin the Sabbath at least twelve hours earlier than we do here. In fact, it takes just forty-eight hours, or the time of two whole days, from the time any one day begins in the extreme east till it ends at the farthest place in the west. Will the reader stop and think carefully, sharply, on this point, for it is an important one? It takes twenty-four hours for the *first end* of a day to go clear around the earth. Then, as the *last end* of the day is twenty-four hours behind the first end, it must also have twenty-four more to go clear around the earth, and that makes forty-eight hours in all that each day is on the earth somewhere. So for the Lord and the heavenly host to keep Sabbath with all the Adventists on earth, they would have to keep the time of two whole days each week. And in that case, those on this side of the earth would be working while the Lord was keeping the Sabbath with those on the other side of the earth; and those on the opposite side of the earth would be working while the Lord was keeping Sabbath with those on this side. Thus, none of them would keep Sabbath with the Lord, after all! In fact, there is not a single hour in the week when there is not some Sabbatarian at work on some part of the earth!

What, then, becomes of Mrs. White's statement that "all the angelic hosts" keep our Sabbath? or Uriah Smith's hypothesis that all the universe "will observe the same period together"? Both are utterly absurd. The same definite seventh day cannot be kept by all the universe; even on this earth alone it cannot be kept by all at the same time. This adds another proof that the seventh day Sabbath with its rigorous limitations and exactions, as enjoined in the law, was only a Jewish institution, to be carried out by a small people, in a limited territory—the land of Canaan. Under the new dispensation, the gospel was to go to all nations, to all climates, around the earth. Hence the keeping of a definite Sabbath Day is left out of the gospel system, the *rest* now enjoyed by Christians being a spiritual rest of the soul, every day of the week.

Test the seventh-day theory in the frozen regions of the north. The law declared that the day must be kept from sunset to sunset (see Lev. 23:32). In the extreme north in the winter there are months when the sun is not seen there at all, so they have no sunset. And again, in summer there are months when the sun is above the horizon all the time, when there is no sunrise. This difficulty confronts the Adventists of northern Sweden and Norway. Here their theory breaks down again. They have to reckon the day by artificial means. This again proves that that law was for the Jews. What endless and needless difficulties people get themselves into trying to keep a law that was designed only for the Jews in a limited locality! How contrary to the freedom and simplicity of the gospel!

Another great difficulty that stands in the way of Sabbatarianism is, *Where shall we begin the day?* If a man's salvation depends upon keeping the same day to the hour that God kept it at creation, then it is infinitely important that we know exactly where his day began, so as to begin ours there too. But the Lord has not said a word about it, nor given the least clue respecting where to begin the day. The day is now generally reckoned to begin at a certain line 180 degrees west from Greenwich, England. It runs north and south through the Pacific Ocean about 4,000 miles west of America.

Prof. E. S. Holden of Lick Observatory says: "There is no one date when the day-line was established there; but it was during the last hundred years. It was established there for convenience. Besides Greenwich, it has been reckoned from Canary Islands, Tenereffe, Ferro, Paris, Berlin, Jerusalem, Washington, etc." So we see: 1. It is only within the last hundred years that the day-line has been fixed where it now is. 2. This was done merely for convenience, not because there was anything in nature requiring it. 3. At different times the day-line has been counted from at least seven different places, from Jerusalem in the east to Washington in the west, about 8,000 miles difference, or one-third the way around the earth. Hence the beginning of the seventh day has varied this much at different times. 4. In another century it may be changed again. 5. There is just as much authority for one place as the other, and no divine authority for either, as it is all man's work and done at haphazard. 6. Hence so far as duty to God is concerned, any nation, church or society is at liberty to begin the day wherever they please. One place will be just as apt to be in harmony with God's day-line as another.

Sabbatarians in America can fix their day-line in the Atlantic instead of in the Pacific, and then our Sunday will be Saturday, and they will be all right and convert a nation in a day!

Indeed, this is exactly parallel to what Seventh-day Adventists have done in the case of a colony in the Pacific Ocean. Pitcairn Island, in the Pacific, was settled one hundred years ago by persons who brought their reckoning eastward from Asia. But it happens to be on the American side of the present day-line; hence their Sunday was our Saturday, and they all kept it one hundred years as Sunday. According to Adventists, this was an awful thing, for Sunday is the Pope's Sabbath, the mark of the beast! So the Adventists went there and persuaded them all to keep Saturday. How? They simply induced them to change their reckoning of the day-line a few miles, and lo! their Sunday was Saturday! Now they are all pious Sabbath-keepers, while before they were keeping Sunday, the mark of the beast! And yet they are keeping exactly the same day they kept before. If this is not hair-splitting, tell me what is. It illustrates the childishness of the whole Sabbatarian business. Now let the Adventists just shift their day-line a little farther east to include America, and they can keep Sunday with the other people. Does the salvation of a man's soul depend upon such mathematical uncertainties as these? If it does, we may well despair of heaven.

The law said keep the seventh day from sunset to sunset (Exod. 20:8-11; Lev. 23:32). Now, let two Adventists start from Chicago, one going east, the other west, around the earth. Each keeps carefully the seventh day as the sun sets. When they meet again at Chicago they will be two days apart! One will be keeping Sunday and the other Friday. How will they now manage it? Each gives up his seventh day, and both take that of the world. So they have only a worldly day, after all.

Look, also, at the difficulty in crossing this supposed day-line in the Pacific Ocean. Going west, a day is dropped going east it is added, and this is done at *noon* of the day which finds them nearest the supposed line. On the vessel, a man going west sits down to dinner 11:50 a. m. Friday. While he is eating the time is changed, and he rises from dinner Saturday noon! Then he has only six hours of Sabbath till sunset. But coming east, he sits down to dinner Saturday noon and rises from dinner Friday noon! He has kept eighteen hours Sabbath; then it is gone in a second at high noon, and he has six hours to work till sunset. Now he must begin Sabbath once more and keep it over again—twenty-four hours. In one case he keeps only six hours Sabbath, and in the other case he keeps forty-two hours!

These stubborn facts demonstrate the utter absurdity of the Sabbatarian view. It proves that the strict keeping of days was confined to the Jews in Palestine.

The Covenant From Sinai

We now come to the Sabbath as instituted in the Ten-Commandment law given on Sinai. With this law the Sabbath either stands or falls.

A covenant was made with the children of Israel "from Sinai, which gendereth to bondage" (Gal. 4:24). Paul terms it the "first covenant" (Heb. 8:7); the "old" covenant (vs. 13). The question, then, to be settled is, What constituted the *old* or *first* covenant which came from Sinai? The Bible answer is clear.

"And Moses rose up early in the morning, and went up unto Mount Sinai, as the Lord had commanded him, and took in his hand the two tables of stone." "And he was there with the Lord forty days and forty nights; he did neither eat bread, nor drink water. And he wrote upon the tables the words of the covenant, the ten commandments" (Exod. 34:4, 28).

"The Lord our God made a covenant with us in Horeb. The Lord made not this covenant with our fathers, but with us....The Lord talked with you face to face in the mount out of the midst of the fire,...saying, [1] Thou shalt have no other gods before me. [2] Thou shalt not make thee any graven image:...thou shalt not bow down thyself unto them, nor serve them.... [3] Thou shalt not take the name of the Lord thy God in vain. [4] Keep the Sabbath Day....The seventh day is the Sabbath.... [5] Honor thy father and thy mother.... [6] Thou shalt not kill. [7] Neither shalt thou commit adultery. [8] Neither shalt thou steal. [9] Neither shalt thou bear false witness.... [10] Neither shalt thou covet....These words spake the Lord unto all your assembly in the mount:....*and he added no more.* And he wrote them in two tables of stone, and delivered them unto me" (Deut. 5:2-22).

"And he declared unto you his covenant, which he commanded you to perform, even Ten Commandments; and he wrote them upon two tables of stone" (Deut. 4:13).

"When I was going up into the mount to receive the tables of stone, even the tables of the covenant which the Lord made with you" (Deut. 9:9). "The Lord gave me the two tables of stone, even the tables of the covenant." (vs. 11).

"The ark, wherein is the covenant of the Lord, which he made with our fathers, when he brought them out of the land of Egypt" (1 Kings 8:21). "There was nothing in the ark save the two tables of stone" (1 Kings 8:9), "the tables of the covenant" (Heb. 9:4).

Comments could not make these texts prove more clearly that the ten commandments were the covenant from Sinai. Eight clear texts declare that that "covenant" was "the Ten Commandments."

I shall next prove that the breaking of any of the Ten Commandments was called breaking the covenant.

"They have forsaken the covenant of the Lord God of their fathers, which he made with them when he brought them forth out of the land of Egypt: for they went and served other gods, and worshipped them" (Deut. 29:25, 26). "This people will rise up, and go a whoring after the gods of strangers...and will forsake me, and break my covenant which I have made with them" (Deut. 31:16).

"And it came to pass, when the judge was dead, that they returned, and corrupted themselves more than their fathers, in following other gods to serve them, and to bow down unto them; ... this people hath transgressed my covenant" (Judges 2:19, 20).

"Ye have transgressed the covenant of the Lord your God,...and have gone and served other gods, and bowed yourselves to them" (Josh. 23:16). Also read 1 Kings 11:9-11; Jer. 11:10; 22:9.

Here we have seven texts which declare that by the children

of Israel's breaking the first commandments of the Decalog they "broke," "forsook," and "transgressed" God's covenant. This proves beyond question that the Decalog was the first covenant; for "the Lord had made a covenant, and charged them, saying, Ye shall not fear other gods, nor bow yourselves to them, nor serve them" (2 Kings 17:35).

Again in 2 Kings 17:15, 16, we read that they made "molten images" and worshipped them, and by so doing rejected "his covenant that he made with their fathers." So by breaking the second commandment of the Decalog they rejected his covenant. "Lest ye forget the covenant of the Lord...and make you a graven image, or the likeness of anything" (Deut. 4:23).

On account of Israel's stealing and coveting, thus breaking the eighth and tenth commandments of the Decalog, God said, "Israel hath sinned, and they have also transgressed my covenant" (Josh. 7:10-12, 21). By breaking the sixth commandment Israel forsook the covenant. (2 Kings 19:9, 10).

Surely the twenty foregoing texts are sufficient to prove that the "Ten Commandments" were the first covenant, the one from Sinai. It must be a desperate case that will cause people to reject these plain statements of the Bible, and look elsewhere for that covenant.

"Therefore it is fixed and settled by all the above quotations, and the concurrence of all other scriptures, that the Sinai covenant embraced the 'ten words' of the stone tables. Now, the law for the seventh-day Sabbath is found in this covenant, written on stone. Therefore every time the Word of God declares that the covenant delivered on Sinai is abolished it asserts the abrogation of the seventh-day Sabbath. And because of the strong array of New Testament scriptures which positively assert the abrogation of that Ten-Commandment covenant made on Sinai, the Adventists have diligently sought out some new device to deny that the Decalog is the covenant which God made with Israel at that time, and to find something else to which they can apply the covenant.

"But let us examine their new invention. Avoiding the

definition that God gives us no less than twenty times, of the covenant that he made on Sinai, they appeal to the dictionary and find this definition: *'Covenant.* A mutual agreement of two or more persons or parties, in writing and under seal,' etc. Then confining the covenant made on Sinai within this single definition, they look for something that answers thereto, or rather they search for something else besides the Ten Commandments to which they may apply those scriptures that declare the abrogation of the old covenant. So in their literature and preaching they light upon Exod. 19:5-8. 'Here,' say they, 'is an agreement between God and the people; and this promise on the part of Israel to do all that God had spoken, is the covenant made on Sinai.'

"An argument is drawn from the fifth verse, which reads thus: 'Now therefore, if ye will obey my voice indeed, and keep my covenant, then ye shall be a peculiar treasure unto me above all people.' The word 'covenant' occurring in the context of the people's promise to obey all that God had spoken, is used to prove that that agreement alone constituted the covenant. U. Smith asserts in a little work that this agreement, and nothing else, was the old covenant, and that nothing else was abolished by the bringing in of the new order under Christ Jesus.

"1. The Word does not assert that the promise of the people to obey God, alone constitutes the covenant made on Sinai. But it is repeatedly declared that the ten words written in the stone tables were included in the covenant made with Israel at that time and place.

"2. If the response on the part of Israel to obey what God had spoken, only was the covenant; and if nothing else, as U. Smith affirms, was abolished in Christ, then the ceremonial laws, and the penalty of death for the violation of the Sabbath, and the other judgments written in the book of the law, are all yet in force.

"3. If that agreement on the part of the people of God to obey him was the covenant, and nothing else, and if that only was done away in Christ, then it follows that in Christ Jesus we cease to be under covenant obligations to obey God."

"The word 'covenant' in Exodus and Deuteronomy referring to the law of God given on Sinai is from *berith* in the Hebrew, and the same thing in the New Testament is from the Greek word *diatheke.* It is translated 'testament' thirteen times. And in the following instances, where rendered 'covenant,' in the margin it is more correctly translated 'testament'; Rom. 9:4; Gal. 3:15; 4:24; Heb. 8:6; 12:24; 13:20. It is seen that in Heb. 9:16 the word is used in the sense of a will, such as men make for the disposition of their property, etc....In Heb. 9:15 the same word is used with reference to both the old and the new testament. If, therefore, *diatheke* simply means a mutual agreement, then the twenty-seven books we have been in the habit of calling the New Testament are not the 'new testament.'

"But let us look at their position again. A covenant is a mutual agreement between two or more parties; therefore the Ten Commandments are not the covenant made on Sinai, because they are not such an agreement. Again, say they, 'The new covenant written in the heart are the Ten Commandments formerly written in stone.' But the same word, *diatheke,* occurs in Heb. 9:15 in speaking of both the old testament and the new. Therefore, if the 'old *diatheke'* cannot be the Ten Commandments because the word means a 'mutual contract,' then, for the same reason, the 'new *diatheke'* cannot be the Ten Commandments. Thus their scheme to overthrow the fact that the old covenant includes the ten stone-written words over-throws their own position that the Decalog is the new covenant.

"Let us now see what the real Scriptural meaning of the word 'covenant' or 'testament' is. *'Testament.* 1. A solemn, authentic instrument in writing, by which a person declares his will as to the disposal of his estate and effects after death. 2. One of the two general divisions of the canonical books of the sacred Scriptures; as, the Old Testament; the New Testament.' These are the only definitions given in Webster's *Unabridged Dictionary.*

"'Diatheke, any disposition, arrangement, institution, or

dispensation: hence a testament, will (Heb. 9:15).— *Greenfield*

"'*Diatheke,* a disposition, arrangement. A testament, a will. The Abrahamic covenant. The Mosaic covenant entered into at Mount Sinai, with sacrifices and the blood of victims (see Exod. 24:3-12; Deut. 5:2). The new covenant, the Gospel Dispensation.'—*Robinson's Lexicon.*

"'Thus, the covenant of Sinai was conditioned by the observance of the Ten Commandments (Exod. 34:27, 28; Lev. 26:15), which are therefore called "Jehovah's covenant" (Deut. 4:13), a name which was extended to all the books of Moses, if not to the whole body of Jewish canonical Scriptures (2 Cor. 3:13, 14). This last-mentioned covenant, which was renewed at different periods, is one of the two principal covenants between God and man. They are distinguished as old and new (Jer. 31:31-34; Heb. 8:8-13; 10: *16).* '—*Smith and Barnum's Dictionary*

"Thus, we see by Scriptural use and standard authorities that the word rendered 'covenant' signifies a 'will,' a 'dispensation,' etc., and the Ten-Commandment covenant is cited as an example. The word is properly used to designate the two general divisions of the Bible. The Decalog, properly speaking, is the old covenant, but as the last authority has truthfully observed, the old testament is also used in an extended sense, as including all the books of Moses, or the entire body of the Sinaitic law.

"We have now proved that the very word 'covenant' in its Scriptural meaning is in perfect accord with the statements of the Almighty when 'he declared unto you his covenant, which he commanded you to perform, even the Ten Commandments; and he wrote them on two tables of stone' (Deut. 4:13). But once more, the Adventist teachers will cry, 'A covenant is an agreement with some one, but such is not the Decalog.' Here is God's answer by Moses: 'When I was gone up info the mount to receive the tables of stone, even the tables of the *covenant which the Lord made with you'* (Deut. 9:9)."

Every effort to exclude the Decalog from the Sinaitic covenant is squarely against the Bible. But let us examine closer. The Decalog did enter into, and become a part of, an *agreement* between the Lord and Israel. The Decalog was the basis of the whole arrangement at Sinai. Therefore, by way of eminence, it alone was frequently called "the covenant."

We open at Exod. 19 and read: "In the third month, when the children of Israel were gone forth out of the land of Egypt, the same day came they into the wilderness of Sinai" (vs. 1). Moses was mediator between the Lord and the children of Israel (see vs. 3). Moses came down and delivered to Israel God's terms. "Now therefore, if ye will obey my voice indeed, and keep my covenant, then ye shall be a peculiar treasure unto me above all people" (vss. 5, 7). The people answered, "All that the Lord hath spoken we will do" (vs. 8). Here was an agreement between God and Israel. They agreed to obey his covenant, and he agreed to bless them.

Next they prepared to hear his voice, to hear the covenant (vss. 9-25). Then chapter 20 begins with God speaking aloud to Israel, and the very first thing heard are the Ten Commandments, extending to verse 17. He then follows the Ten Commandments with various precepts through Moses, to the end of chapter 23. "Moses came and told the people *all the words* of the Lord." "And all the people answered with one voice, and said, All the words which the Lord hath said will we do" (chap. 24:3). Then "Moses wrote all the words of the Lord" in a book, verse 4, and that book was called "the book of the covenant" (vs. 7).

"And he took the book of the covenant, and read in the audience of the people: and they said, All that the Lord hath said will we do, and be obedient. And Moses took the blood, and sprinkled it on the people, and said, Behold the blood of the covenant which the Lord hath made with you concerning all these words" (Exod. 24:7, 8).

That closed the covenant. It embraced all included in the record from Exod. 19:1 to Exod. 24:8, for this is the covenant in detail written out. It was a testament, disposition, arrangement; and an agreement between God and the Israelites. But is the Decalog included in it? Adventists might as well deny that the sun shines. It is written out in full in the covenant (Exod. 20:1-

17); and the seventh-day Sabbath is in its very heart (vss. 8-11). We are sure that this was the first or old covenant. Paul quotes Exod. 24:7, 8, and says it was "the first covenant" (see Heb. 9:18-20). That settles it.

The Decalog was such a prominent part of the covenant that the stones on which it was written were called "the tables of the covenant" (Deut. 9:9), the book in which it was written was called "the book of the covenant" (Exod. 24:7); and the ark in which it was deposited was called "the ark of the covenant" (Deut. 31:26).

All Saturday-keepers rest their claims for the observance of that day upon the Decalog. But the Decalog was a prominent part of the "old" or Sinaitic covenant. With that covenant the seventh-day Sabbath stands or falls; for there is no possible chance for the law-teachers to take their Sabbath out of the first covenant, made on Sinai. The enjoining of the observance of that day lies in the very heart of that covenant. If the code is in force, the seventh day is in force, for that is the day specified in it; but if that enactment of Jehovah's was superseded by the new testament, in this dispensation, then the seventh day is abolished.

Uriah Smith (leading Adventist) says in his book entitled *Two Covenants,* page 5, "If the Ten Commandments constituted the old covenant, then they are forever gone." The Bible declares in so many words that "the words of the covenant, the Ten Commandments," is the very covenant God made with Israel "when he brought them out of the land of Egypt" (Exod. 34:28; 1 Kings 8:9, 21). Then, the Ten Commandments constituted, or were included in, the old covenant, and "are forever gone."

The Covenant From Sinai Abolished

"Tell me, ye that desire to be under the law, do ye not hear the law? For it is written, that Abraham had two sons, the one by a bondmaid, and the other by a free-woman. But he who was of the bondwoman was born after the flesh; but he of the freewoman was by promise. Which things are an allegory: for these are the two covenants; the one from the Mount Sinai, which gendereth to bondage, which is Agar [Hagar]....But Jerusalem which is above is free, which is the mother of us all....Now we, brethren, as Isaac was, are the children of promise. But as then he that was born after the flesh persecuted him that was born of the Spirit, even so it is now. Nevertheless what saith the scripture? Cast out the bondwoman and her son: for the son of the bondwoman shall not be heir with the son of the freewoman. So then, brethren, we are not children of the bondwoman, but of the free" (Gal. 4:21-31).

Some of the Galatian brethren had become "bewitched" (3:1) through false teaching, and believed it necessary to be circumcised and to "keep the law of Moses." They, like their modern brethren, "observed days" (4:10), and became "entangled with the yoke of bondage." To them is directed this entire Epistle of solemn warnings and powerful arguments against the doctrine that the law system is in force in this dispensation. Because they gave heed to some law-teachers, who "perverted the gospel of Christ" (1:7), and in obedience to their teaching observed law "days," etc., the apostle addressed them, "O foolish Galatians, ...are ye so foolish?"

In the foregoing scripture the apostle uses a powerful argument to show the abrogation of the law system. This he does by an allegory. The four principal characters in this allegory are Hagar, Ishmael, Sarah, and Isaac. These two women, Hagar and Sarah, represent *"two covenants."* Hagar represents the covenant made or given on "Mount Sinai, which gendereth to bondage." Sarah represents the covenant from Jerusalem—"the truth which came by Jesus Christ," which makes men free. The two Sons of one father (Abraham) represent the children of the two covenants: Ishmael, the Jews; and Isaac, the Christians—both Jews and Gentiles.

Mark this fact, that the covenant from Sinai is denominated a *"bondwoman,"* and all who cling to that covenant are her "children." "Ye that desire to be under the law." This applies to all Saturday-keepers. "Do ye not hear the law?" What law? Answer: The "covenant, the one from Mount Sinai, which gendereth to bondage, which is Hagar." The Sinaitic covenant was "bondage," and the apostle warned them to "be not entangled again with the yoke of bondage" (chap. 5:1). "What saith the scripture? *Cast out the bondwoman and her son.*" Language could not be framed to teach more clearly the abrogation of the old covenant. "So then, brethren, we are not children of the bondwoman, but of the free." Not under the Sinaitic covenant, but under the new covenant of grace in Christ Jesus. "These two covenants do not mix or blend together in the same heart, nor in the same dispensation." To accept Christ in his fullness is to cast out Hagar and her Sabbath.

"But *now* hath he obtained a more excellent ministry, by how much also he is the mediator of a better covenant, which was established upon better promises. For if that first covenant had been faultless, then should no place have been sought for the second. For finding fault with them, he saith, Behold, the days come, saith the Lord, when I will make a new covenant with the house of Israel and with the house of Judah: not according to the covenant that I made with their fathers in the day when I took them by the hand to lead them out of the land of Egypt; because they continued not in my covenant, and I regarded them not, saith the Lord. For this is the covenant that I will make with the house of Israel after those days, saith the Lord; I will put my laws into their mind, and write them in their hearts: and I will be to them a God, and they shall be to me a people: and they shall not teach every man his neighbor, and every man his brother, saying, Know the Lord: for all shall know me, from the least to the greatest. For I will be merciful to their unrighteousness, and their sins and their iniquities will I remember no more. In that he saith, A new covenant, he hath made the first old. Now that which decayeth and waxeth old is ready to vanish away" (Heb. 8:6-13).

Here the two covenants are clearly contrasted. The one from Sinai is termed "the first covenant," "old covenant," "faulty" covenant, which "decayeth," "waxeth old," and "is ready to vanish away." That ends the old covenant, the one from Sinai, the ten commandments, as we have proved. But the new testament is termed the "second covenant," "new covenant," "better covenant," "not according to" the first, "written in our minds and hearts." There is no way to evade this plain testimony.

Paul says that God made the first with Israel—"in the day when I took them by the hand to lead them out of the land of Egypt." "Now, what covenant did God make with Israel after their exodus? Here is a perfect answer: 'And I have set there a place for the ark, *wherein is the covenant of the Lord, which he made with our fathers, when he brought them out of the land of Egypt'* (1 Kings 8:21). It was that which Moses deposited in the ark; i. e., 'the tables of the covenant' (Heb. 9:4). And turning back to 1 Kings 8, we read in verse 9, *'There was nothing in the ark save the two tables of stone,* which Moses put there at Horeb, when the Lord made a covenant with the children of Israel, when they came out of the land of Egypt.'

"So, then, Jeremiah tells us that the former covenant was that which God made with Israel when he took them by the hand to lead them out of Egypt, and that was the covenant which he wrote on tables of stone and put in the ark. There is no possible evading the truth here.

"After quoting the very scriptures above cited, U. Smith, in his tract on *The Two Covenants* says, 'They ask us, "What can be plainer? There was nothing in the ark but the two tables of stone, containing the Ten Commandments: yet Solomon says that in the ark was the covenant which the Lord made with the fathers of his people, when he brought them out of the land of Egypt. Therefore those commandments were the covenant." And having established this point, they have but to quote Paul's testimony, that the old covenant has waxed old, and vanished away, to reach the conclusion so long and anxiously sought, that the Ten Commandments have been abolished, carrying with them the obnoxious seventh-day Sabbath into their eternal tomb.

"Yes, we do humbly ask in the name of all reason, What can be plainer than the positive, unequivocal statements of the Bible, especially where it is emphatically and repeatedly declared that

the tables of stone were included in the covenant made with the
Israelites at Sinai when they came out of Egypt? Indeed, were we
to disbelieve all these scriptures, how could we credit the Bible
at all? Accepting the inspired record, it is settled forever that the
first covenant included the Decalog, which 'is ready to vanish
away.' 'Is nigh disappearing.'—Young's *Translatton.* 'Abolished.'—*Thomson.*

"Therefore all the disputers of the gospel of Christ, and vain
janglers for the law of Moses, are clinging to an old decayed
system that in God's order vanished away [over] nineteen
hundred years ago. And all these modern folks are as zealous as
their ancient brethren—compassing land and sea, not to convert
men to Christ, but to put upon them the yoke of the law, which
they themselves cannot bear. Surely this is *Nehushtan—a piece
of brass.*

"God directed Moses to make a brazen serpent in the
wilderness. It was all right for its object. But 765 years after that
we find idolatrous Israel worshiping that serpent. But King
Hezekiah, we are told, 'removed the high places, and brake the
images, and cut down the groves, and brake in pieces the brazen
serpent that Moses had made: for unto those days the children of
Israel did burn incense to it: and he called it Nehushtan' (2 Kings
18:4).

"What is the difference between the worship of that serpent,
and the worship of those who in many cases actually make a god
out of that Sabbath, which, though it was appointed of God for a
certain purpose and time, as the brazen serpent also had its use,
has passed away, in the order of his will?

"Doubtless, those ancient worshipers reasoned just as the
modern ones do: 'God is immutable, unchangeable, therefore his
laws are unchangeable. But "we know that God spake to Moses,"
commanding the children of Israel to look up to this serpent;
therefore we will continue to look to it forever.'

'Then said he, Lo, I come to do thy will, O God. *He taketh
away the first, that he may establish the second.* By the which
will Testament we are sanctified, through the offering of the

body of Jesus Christ once for all' (Heb. 10:9, 10). Praise God! The Spirit gives us these words as a present testimony. *We are sanctified.*

"Two covenants are set in comparison all the way through this Epistle, called the 'first covenant,' and the 'second.' The former is very commonly called 'the law.' And here we reach the same end of the first covenant to which we have been brought time and again in the inspired Epistles. Christ himself, and not Constantine, nor the Pope of Rome, 'took away the first' covenant, and established the second, his own perfect law. And with this change ends the Mosaic Sabbath.

"There are two positions upon which the 'teachers of the law' usually shift, in order to dodge the Word of God; namely, one time they admit that the law, the old covenant, is abolished, but it means only the ceremonial part; and when driven from that, they change their position, and say, 'We are only delivered from the law by obeying it through grace; that is, "from the curse of the law."' But the Word of God emphatically declares the passing away of the whole legal economy. The word 'testament' is defined as a 'complete arrangement, or dispensation.' So when Christ 'took away the first, that he might establish the second,' there was a complete dispensational change of the law, the setting up of an entirely new divine order and government. Christ is the 'Mediator of the new testament,' which has superseded the entire old economy, which was given to the Israelites on Mount Sinai.

"And one small phrase, in the midst of this inspired treatise on the abrogation of the old covenant, and the establishing of the new by Christ, is sufficient to prove that the apostle meant by the first covenant, of which he so frequently speaks, just what it was called when first given; namely, these words: 'and the tables of the covenant' (Heb. 9:4). Here the Sabbath of the Jews, and the heresy of the Ebionites must die, being thrust through with the 'Sword of the Spirit.' The old covenant, which was 'ready to vanish away' (8:13), is familiarly spoken of in connection with the tables of the covenant. Paul was well posted in the Old

Testament, and knew very well that God 'wrote upon the tables the words of the covenant, the Ten Commandments' (Exod. 34:28), and had given to Moses 'the two tables of stone, even the tables of the covenant' (Deut. 9:11). And he surely must have known that after speaking of the old covenant vanishing away, and then of 'the tables of the covenant,' in the same connection, all would naturally understand him as teaching that the covenant written on stones was abolished."—*The Sabbath.*

Again, the two covenants are contrasted in Heb. 12:18-29, as follows:

1.   "Ye are not come unto the mount that might be touched, and that burned with fire, nor unto blackness, and darkness, and tempest, and the sound of a trumpet, and the voice of words," etc.; namely, when God came down on Mount Sinai and delivered the law. "That which was commanded," "that which was spoken on earth," that which is *"shaken"* and *"removed."*

2.   "Ye are come unto Mount Zion....The heavenly Jerusalem...to the general assembly and church of the first-born" (the law which came out of Zion, the New Testament), "new covenant," "which speaketh better things," which was spoken "from heaven" (see Heb. 1:1, 2), which *"cannot be shaken"* and *"remains."*

I quote from Canright:

"Adventists are always dwelling upon the terrible scenes at Sinai at the giving of the law, and pointing others there; but Paul says, No, do not go there; but to Mount Zion, to Jesus and the new covenant.

"So Jeremiah predicted the rejection of the covenant in the ark, and that instead of it, men would seek to the name of the Lord at Jerusalem where the gospel went forth. 'In those days, saith the Lord, they shall say no more, The ark of the covenant of the Lord: neither shall it come to mind: neither shall they remember it; neither shall they visit it; neither shall that be done any more. At that time they shall call Jerusalem the throne of the Lord; and all nations shall be gathered unto it, to the name of the

Lord' (Jer. 3:16, 17)."

'Adventists are trying to revive the very thing the Lord said should be forgotten, "the ark of the covenant." Their study and worship is centered around that just as of old with the Jews. But their effort is vain. God has said it. Since the cross, Jesus, and Jerusalem (the church) are where all eyes are turned, while the ark and old covenant are forgotten.'

"Forasmuch as ye are manifestly declared to be the epistle of Christ ministered by us, written not with ink, but with the Spirit of the living God; not in tables of stone, but in fleshly tables of the heart. And such trust have we through Christ to Godward: not that we are sufficient of ourselves to think anything as of ourselves; but our sufficiency is of God; who also hath made us able ministers of the new testament; not of the letter, but of the spirit: for the letter killeth, but the spirit giveth life. But if the ministration of death, written and engraven in stones, was glorious, so that the children of Israel could not steadfastly behold the face of Moses for the glory of his countenance; which glory was to be done away: how shall not the ministration of the spirit be rather glorious? For if the ministration of condemnation be glory, much more doth the ministration of righteousness exceed in glory. For even that which was made glorious had no glory in this respect, by reason of the glory that excelleth. For if that which is done away was glorious, much more that which remaineth is glorious.

"Seeing then that we have such hope, we use great plainness of speech: and not as Moses, which put a vail over his face, that the children of Israel could not stedfastly look to the end of that which is abolished: but their minds were blinded: for unto this day remaineth the same vail untaken away in the reading of the old testament; which vail is done away in Christ" (2 Cor. 3:3-14). Here we have the two covenants contrasted in unmistakable language. The first is defined as "the old testament"; "the ministration of death," which "was glorious"; the letter," which "killeth"; "the ministration of condemnation"; that which "was written and engraven in stones," which is *"done away"* and *"abolished."* The second he terms "the new testament"; "the spirit," which "giveth life" (for comments, see Rom. 8:2; John 6:63); the "ministration of the Spirit"; the "ministration of righteousness"; the "glory that excelleth"; that which is "written in the fleshly tables of the heart," and "remaineth."

"No other testament law-teacher is sent of God. In the present dispensation, He only makes men 'ministers of the new testament.' It is called the 'ministration of the Spirit'; therefore no one can receive or teach it without the gift of the Holy Spirit, excepting in the letter, which 'killeth.'

"In verse 7 the ten words are called, 'The ministration of death, written and engraven in stones.' And though it was declared 'glorious,' it was 'done away.' 'For if that which *is done away* was glorious [the law written on stones, see verse 7], much more that which remaineth is glorious' (vs. 11). 'That which remaineth' is the new testament, of which God made Paul an 'able minister.' And not as Moses, which put a vail over his face, that the children of Israel could not look stedfastly to the end of that which is *'abolished.'* The abolished law, we are told, was given through Moses, who at the time had his face vailed. Now turn to Exod. 34:28-33, and you will see that it was when he came down from the mount with the covenant in his hands that his face shone, and was vailed.

"In verse 14 the abolished law is plainly declared to be the 'old testament.' The old testament and the old covenant are the same thing. And though we have seen that it is strictly defined as the Ten Commandments, yet these being the statute basis of the entire old book, the whole volume is sometimes called the old *diatheke*—testament.

"On verse 13 we observe, If it were possible for any one to have always performed all moral duty, that person would stand in the highest glory of the law—justified. To this summit of legal glory we are raised by the first work of gospel grace. And then with 'open face'—having left reading Moses—beholding the glory of the Lord in the glass of his Word, 'we are changed into the same image [the complete image of Christ], from glory to glory, even as by the Spirit of the Lord.' We are changed from glory of justification, the highest point of legal glory, to the glory of perfect holiness, which is the summit of gospel grace. 'By the which will we are sanctified.' Thus the second will places us far beyond where the first will could, even if we had kept it. And it is also the perfect and only law by which to live in this mount of new testament holiness.

"We can scarcely conceive how it were possible to employ words that more explicitly assert the abolition of that covenant which was written in the tables of stone. If we were to admit the division of the law into two laws, as the Adventists contend, and were held to prove that one of those laws was abolished, we certainly should find more abundant proof to dispose of that written on stone than of the ceremonial part. The reason is obvious. The former constituting the real covenant, the statutes of that nation, to which the latter were appended, it was only necessary to remove the statute basis, and, of course, all the rest goes with it....And how very specific and unmistakable this language in 2 Cor. 3. All Bible readers know that nothing but the ten commandments were written in the stone tables, and it is affirmed that the very thing that had been 'written and engraven in stones' is abolished, and done away. Compare verses 7 and 11.

"With this and similar scriptures the law-teachers have no little trouble. They find themselves even in open hostility to the truth. What can they do? One says to us, 'It was not the law, but "the ministration of death"; i. e., the annexed penalty of death for its violation.' But the inspired testimony is that it was that which was written and engraven in stone, which was only the ten prohibitory laws, and not the penalties of death for their violation. So Mr. Adventist is bound by the Word of God; and the Scriptures cannot be broken. But let us look at that theory. Two things are set in contrast in this lesson. The first is called, 'the ministration of death,' 'the ministration of condemnation,' 'the old testament' (vss. 7, 9, 14). The second is called, the 'ministration of the Spirit,' 'the ministration of righteousness,' 'the new testament' (vss. 8, 9, 5). The former was written in stones; the latter is received by the Spirit, which is shed abroad in our hearts. The former is 'abolished,' 'is done away' (vss. 13, 11). The latter is 'that which remaineth' (vs. 11). So the old testament is done away, and the new testament, of which Christ is mediator, remains in force.

"But the old had a degree of glory notwithstanding it was 'the ministration of death.'…The stone laws were glorious, 'so that the children of Israel could not steadfastly behold the face of Moses for the glory of his countenance' (vs. 7). This was when he came down with the tables of the law in his hands. And it is also the 'ministration of death,' because death followed its violation. To minister, is to give; ministration, the act of giving. In Gal. 3:21 we are told the law could not 'have given life.' But, on the contrary, it could give death. Therefore in it was both glory and the ministration of death. But its glory was 'done away,' and also the thing itself that was glorious 'is abolished.'"
—*The Sabbath.*

With the abolition of the Sinaitic covenant, the seventh-day Sabbath was taken away; for it lay in the heart of the abolished covenant.

Smith's Two Covenants[2]

"The very first transaction we find taking place between God and the Israelites after they left Egypt which answers to the definition of the word 'covenant,' must be the first covenant, unless some good reason can be shown why it is not."

So saying, U. Smith lights upon Exod. 19:7, 8, and calls the promise of the people there to obey God's voice the covenant, and nothing more. Now we propose to give five very good reasons why that covenant comprehended more than the simple agreement.

First, Mr. Smith does not bring forward one single passage of Scripture in which that agreement alone is pointed out as the

---

[2] From *The Sabbath*

"first covenant" or the old covenant.

Our second very good reason for believing that Smith's new discovery in Exod. 19:7, 8, alone is not the covenant that God made with Israel when he brought them out of Egypt, is this: The Scriptures positively declare that the covenant then made was the Ten Commandments that were written in stone.

1st proof-text, Exod. 34:28.

2nd proof-text, Deut. 5:3-22.

3rd proof-text, Deut. 4:13.

4th proof-text, Deut. 9:9.

5th proof-text, Deut. 9:11.

6th proof-text, Deut. 9:15.

7th proof-text, 1 Kings 8:21.

8th proof-text, Heb. 9:4.

These eight direct and positive statements of the Bible, besides many indirect proofs, are, we hope, a sufficient apology for not believing Mr. Smith's contrary theory.

Our third reason is based upon the fact that Mr. Smith himself says, page 8, "That the Ten Commandments are called a covenant we admit." With this concession, and the fact that it was made at the very time Jeremiah says that the old covenant was made, which Paul said had vanished away, I should think myself very foolish to accept his opposite theory unsupported by one direct proof-text.

Our fourth reason is this: A hundred things in the Bible might be picked on for which just as plausible a line of reasoning and arguments could be fabricated as that produced by Mr. Smith for his device. But let every mouth be silent before the Bible, yea, "let God be true and every man a liar."

An argument against God's description of the covenant is taken from Exod. 24:6-8, 12 and Heb. 8:17-20, and thus summed up: "Before Moses was called up to receive this law of Ten Commandments, which God had written, the first covenant had been made, closed up, finished, and ratified by the shedding of the blood. These facts throw a fortification around this point which it is not possible either to break or scale. The first covenant was dedicated with blood. But when that dedication took place, the Ten Commandments, in visible form, had not been put into the possession of the people; they had no copy of them; hence they were not dedicated with blood. Therefore, the Ten Commandments were not the old covenant" (p. 14).

We have only to attend to the Word of God to prove this boasted fortress is chaff, which the hail of truth shall sweep away. Reader, open your Bible and read in Exod. 19:16-19, and you will find that God had already come down upon Sinai in awful majesty,—"thunders and lightning, thick cloud, and the voice of a trumpet exceeding loud," etc.

But the Lord sent Moses down to charge the people to keep outside the prescribed bounds of the mount, lest they should perish (vs. 21). Then chapter 20 begins with the voice of God speaking aloud to all the camp of Israel, and the very first things heard are the Ten Commandments, extending to verse 17. "And all the people saw the thunderings, and the lightnings, and the noise of the trumpet and the mountain smoking," and requested that God would not speak to them, lest they should die; but that Moses would be their mediator (vss. 18, 19). Then the Lord instructed Moses concerning an altar and sacrifices, to the close of the chapter. Chapter 21 begins a long line of laws called "judgments," extending to chapter 23:13. Then follows national feasts, and promises, etc. And in chapter 24:4 we read, *"And Moses wrote all the words of the Lord,* and rose up early in the morning, and builded an altar." "And he took the *book of the covenant,* and read it in the audience of the people: and they said, All that the Lord hath said will we do, and be obedient. And Moses took the blood, and sprinkled it on the people, and said, Behold the blood of the covenant, which the Lord hath made with you concerning all these words" (vss. 7, 8).

Now, if Moses "wrote all the words of the Lord," he wrote the Ten Commandments also, for it cannot be denied that the Lord had already spoken them. You see, dear reader, Mr. Smith's theory would require some parentheses foisted into the text, making the scripture read as follows: "And Moses wrote all

the words of the Lord—excepting the Ten Commandments";
"All that the Lord hath said will we do—excepting the Ten
Commandments"; for Smith says they were not included in the
book of the covenant.

It is a strange thing indeed that Moses would pass by the
most solemn and awful words that God had spoken, and not
write them. But he did write them. There is no supposition in the
case. Happily, that "book of the covenant," which Moses
dedicated with blood, is still extant. Nor is it hid away as a
sacred relic in some foreign museum; but, thank God, a copy of
it lies open before our eyes. And in it we read the Ten
Commandments recorded as the very first thing in Exodus 20,
after which follow other laws, which Mr. Smith calls the
covenant, leaving out the very part that God specially calls the
covenant. Indeed, it would appear that the writer had forgotten
that people generally are blessed with the Bible and can read it.
He says that at the time of dedication of the book of the covenant
(Exod. 24:7, 8), "the Ten Commandments, in visible form, had
not been put into the possession of the people; they had no copy
of them." But turning back to chapter 20, we find that one of the
first things in that book of laws given on Sinai is a copy of the
Ten Commandments. God had spoken them; and before the
dedication of the volume, "Moses wrote all the words of the
Lord" (Exod. 24:4).

And as Paul words it, "When Moses had spoken every
precept to all the people, according to the law, he took the blood
of calves,...saying, This is the blood of the testament [the same
as covenant] which God hath enjoined on you" (Heb. 9:19, 20).
The fact that the Ten Commandments constitute the covenant,
and are the first part and foundation of the whole book of the
law, is just the reason why it was denominated "the book of the
covenant." "Every precept according to the law," includes the
ten precepts. Paul says that Moses spoke them. But turning back
to Exod. 24:7, we see that he read them out of the book which he
had written.

So after the whole book of the law had been given, Moses

was called up again on the mountain, and God gave him tables of stone in which was a copy of the Ten Commandments (Exod. 24:12), following which he gave him directions concerning the tabernacle and all its appurtenances, priestly robes, sacrifices, the altar, layer, etc., extending to chapter 32. There Moses was informed of the idolatry of the people, and told to go down to them. When he saw the golden calf, he threw down the two tables and broke them (chap. 32:19). Later he hewed two tables like the first, and went up into the presence of God on the mount (chapter 34:4). "And the Lord said unto Moses, Write thou these words: for after the tenor of these words I have made a covenant with thee and with Israel. And he was there with the Lord forty days and forty nights; he did neither eat bread, nor drink water. And he wrote upon the tables the words of the covenant, the Ten Commandments" (Exod. 34:27, 28). What can be more conclusive? He declared the contents of the first tables the covenant. And in repeating the same, he says, "After the tenor of these words I have made a covenant with thee and with Israel." What utter folly to deny the Word of God! So the props fall, one after another, from the Adventist structure, as the hammer of truth strikes them, and light exposes their fallacy.

Speaking of the ten precepts of the covenant, Smith says, "They are never called *the* covenant, referring to the first or old covenant." They are called *"the* covenant," in Exod. 34:28; Deut. 9:9, 11; 1 Kings 8:21; Heb. 9:4. Here he contradicts the Word again.

The "darkness" of Sinai hangs over all their writings. Two more points, directly bearing on this covenant question, we shall notice. Alluding to the death of the old and the introduction of the new covenant, in Jer. 31:31, 32 and Heb. 8, "I will put my laws into their minds, and write them in their hearts." This, he says, was the "law of God in the days of Jeremiah." If it does not mean this, then it should read, "I will put a *new* law into their minds, and write it in their hearts." Does it say, "I will write the old law in their hearts?" No, but it does say, "I will make a new covenant with the house of Israel." "This shall be the covenant I will make: I will put my laws in their inward parts," the law contained in the new covenant, of course. For we are told there was "a *change of* the law." When the new covenant was confirmed in Christ, 'He took away the first that he might establish the second' (Heb. 10:9). He took away the old, which was written in "tables of stone," that he might write the new in "fleshly tables of the heart" (see 2 Cor. 3:3).

The Law

Sabbatarians are continually preaching, talking, writing, and arguing about "the law." Yet in all the New Testament, while we have "preach the kingdom" eight times, "preach the word" seventeen times, "preach Christ" twenty-three times, "preach the gospel" fifty times, not once is It said "preach the law," or "preach the Sabbath"; but Paul boldly declares that all those who desire to be teachers of the law understand "neither what they say, nor whereof they affirm" (1 Tim. 1:7). This is really the truth. A clear comprehension of the law will convince all intelligent minds that modern Sabbath worshipers have not a peg in Scripture upon which to hang their doctrine. We shall consider the subjects under several propositions. I quote from Canright:

Proposition 1. "The law" embraces the whole Mosaic law, moral, civil, and ceremonial.

The term, "the law," when used with the definite article and without qualifying words, refers "in nine cases out of ten, to the Mosaic law, or to the Pentateuch."— *Smith's Bible Dictionary,* Art. Law. Invariably the Adventists use the term "the law" for the Ten Commandments only. They hang up a chart of the Decalog and constantly point to it as "the law" (Matt. 5:17); "the law of the Lord" (Ps. 19:7); "the law of God" (Rom. 7:22). This is their fundamental error on the law. I affirm that "the law" included the whole system of law given to the Israelites at Sinai, embracing all those requirements, whether moral, civil, or ceremonial, Decalog and all. Look at the term "law," in a concordance, or in any Bible lexicon, dictionary, or encyclopedia. "The law" commonly included the whole of the five books of Moses. Even Butler (Adventist) is compelled to make this confession: "The term, 'the law,' among the Jews generally included the five books of Moses, thus including the whole system, moral, ritual, typical, and civil."—*Law in Galatians,* page 70. That is the truth exactly.

Now, bear in mind this one simple fact wherever you find the term "the law," and you will have no trouble with Sabbatarian arguments on "the law."

Take a few examples of the use of the term "the law" (1 Cor. 14:34). Women "are commanded to be under obedience, as also saith *the law.*" Where does the law say this? Gen. 3:16. So Genesis is in the law. Again: "The law had said, Thou shalt not covet" (Rom. 7:7). Where? Exod 20:17. So Exodus is in the law. Once more: "Master, which is the greatest commandment in the law?" (Matt. 22:36). Jesus then makes two quotations from the law: First, "Thou shalt love the Lord with all thy heart." This is taken from Deut. 6:5. So Deuteronomy is in the law. Second, "Thou shalt love thy neighbor as thyself." This is from Lev. 19:18. So Leviticus is a part of the law. And this: "Have ye not read in the law, how that on the Sabbath Days the priests in the temple profane the Sabbath and are blameless?" (Matt. 12:5). It is from Num. 28:9. These, then, embrace all the five books of Moses as *"the law."* Observe a little where the law is spoken of and you will soon see that it refers indiscriminately to each and all the books of Moses as "the law." Of course, any verse in any of these books is quoted as "the law," because it is a part of the law. So the Ten Commandments are quoted as the law because they are a part of the law.

Again, "the law" embraces all parts of the law, moral, civil, or ceremonial. Thus the ceremonial precepts: "The parents brought in the child Jesus to do with him after the custom of the law" (Luke 2:27). That is, to offer a sacrifice (vs. 24). Moral precepts: "The law is not made for a righteous man, but for the lawless and disobedient, for the ungodly and for sinners, for unholy and profane, for murderers" (1 Tim. 1:9). This is the

Decalog. Civil precepts: "Commandest me to be smitten contrary to the law?" (Acts 23:3). Notice that every time it is simply "the law." "Gamaliel, a doctor of the law" (Acts 5:34). Of what law? Every intelligent man knows that the law of which he was doctor or teacher, was the whole Pentateuch, Decalog included. The law, then, is the whole Jewish law, in all its parts. This one point, clearly settled, destroys nine-tenths of all the Seventh-Day Adventist argument for the Jewish Sabbath.

Proposition 2. There was no such thing as two separate laws given to the Jews.

To sustain their doctrine, Sabbatarians have invented a theory of two laws given at Sinai; one the moral law, the other the ceremonial.

Adventists attach the utmost importance to their theory of two laws, as well they may; for if this is wrong their cause is lost. U. Smith says: "No question, therefore, more vital to the interest of Sabbath keepers can be proposed."—Synopsis *of Present Truth,* page 258. But that they are wrong on this vital question is very easily shown.

"Moral law," "ceremonial law." Adventists use these two terms as freely as though the Bible were full of them; yet, strange to say, the Scriptures make no such distinctions, and never once do we read of "moral" law and "ceremonial" law in the Bible. The place to find these terms is in Adventist literature. In the Bible the Old Testament is simply called "the law." Had the primitive Christians stood on the Adventist platform, when Paul and Christ were preaching concerning "the law," they would have been frequently interrupted with "What law?" "What law?" "The ceremonial or the moral?" But such questions were never asked, for all knew of but one law—the Pentateuch. Adventists severely criticize those who happen to use an unscriptural word or phrase; yet they themselves do that thing commonly, as in this case. It would be amusing to hear one of them try to preach on the "two laws" and confine himself to Bible language. He could not possibly do it. If there were two distinct laws given to Israel, so different in their nature, it is

strange that there is no record of it, no reference to it in the Bible. If one was abolished and the other was not, strange that Paul should not make the distinction when he has so much to say about the law. Why did he not say, "we establish the moral law?" or "the ceremonial law was our schoolmaster"? No, he just says "the law," and leaves it there. He seems not to have been quite as clear on that point as Adventists are! "Neither Christ nor the apostle ever distinguished between the moral, the ceremonial, and the civil law, when they spoke of its establishment or its abolition."—Kitto's *Cyclopedia of Biblical Literature,* —Art. Law.

Adventists have drawn up a long list of things which they claim are true of what they call the "moral law" and an opposite list which they apply to their "ceremonial law." These two they contrast and make out two laws. Thus U. Smith: "Moral law":— "Was spoken from Sinai by the voice of God and twice written upon tables of stone by his own finger. Was deposited in the golden ark. Related only to moral duties."—*Synopsis of Present Truth,* page 266. Of course, this was just the Ten Commandments, nothing more, nothing less. So here we have their "moral law." Now here is the other one: "The ceremonial law": "Was communicated to Moses privately and was by Moses written with a pen in a book (Deut. 31:9)." "Was put into a receptacle by the side of the ark (Deut. 31:26)." "Was wholly ceremonial" (same page).

Hence everything not found in the Decalog belongs to the ceremonial law, and everything Moses himself wrote in the book of the law placed in the side of the ark is "wholly ceremonial." Deut. 31:26 reads: "Take this book of the law and put it in the side of the ark." We inquire, then, how much "the book of the law" contained. The answer is easy: It contained all the five books of Moses—Genesis, Exodus, Leviticus, Numbers, and Deuteronomy. Thus 2 Kings 14:6 says it "is written in the book of the law of Moses," and then quotes Deut. 24:16, as the book of the law. 2 Chron. 35:12 says: "It is written in the book of Moses," and refers to Lev. 3:3. Ezra 6:18 says: "It is written in

the book of Moses," and refers to Num. 3:6. Josh. 8:31 quotes
Exod. 20:25, as that which "is written in the book of the law." 1
Cor. 14:34 refers to Gen. 3:16, as "the law." This settles beyond
question that the book of the law deposited in the side of the ark
was the five books of Moses. Dr. Scott on Deut. 31:26 says:
"This [book] appears to have been a correct and authentic copy
of the five books of Moses."

This book, Adventists say, is "wholly ceremonial." It is
their *ceremonial law.* Yet that very book contained scores of
precepts as purely moral as any in the Decalog. Read these:
"Thou shalt not vex a stranger." "Ye shall not afflict any widow
or fatherless child" (Exod. 22:21, 22). "Thou shalt not follow a
multitude to do evil" (Exod. 23:2). "Ye shall be holy." "Thou
shalt not go up and down as a talebearer among thy people."
"Thou shalt not avenge nor bear any grudge against the children
of thy people, but thou shalt love thy neighbor as thyself" (Lev.
19:2, 16, 18). "Thou shalt not respect persons." "Thou shalt be
perfect" (Deut. 16:19; 18:13). These are but a few among scores
of moral precepts not found in the tables of stone, but in the book
of the law. Are all these to be classed ceremonial because God
did not write them on a stone, but gave them to Moses to write in
a book? Surely not. Then, the nature of a precept was not
determined by the way it was given. God gave them all at
different times as it pleased him.

"The law" embraces the "whole law" (Gal. 5:3). Of course,
in that law, some precepts refer to moral duties, others to civil,
and others to ceremonial; but all are only different parts of the
same law, called, as a whole, "the law." Thus, Jesus quotes from
Leviticus 19, as "the law" (Matt. 22:36-40). Now read the whole
chapter, Leviticus 19, and you find moral, civil, and ceremonial
precepts all mingled together, and often in the same verse.

Another thought: The "book of the law," which U. Smith
calls "wholly ceremonial," contains the Ten Commandments
word for word twice repeated (Exod. 20 and Deut. 5). G. I.
Butler (Adventist) himself makes this concession: "The book of
the law, which was placed in the side of the ark, or at the side of

it, contained both the moral and ceremonial laws."—Law *in Galatians,* page 39. That drops the bottom out of their theory that the moral law was "in the ark, and the ceremonial law in the side of the ark."

On close examination, every text on which they rely for two laws will fail them. That the "book of the law" did contain moral precepts is settled by Gal. 3:10: "It is written, Cursed is every one that continueth not in all things which are written in the book of the law to do them" Where in the book of the law is this written? In Deut. 27:26. Turning there, we have a curse against images (vs. 15); disobedience to parents (vs. 16); adultery (vs. 20); murder (vs. 24); bribery (vs. 25); then comes the verse quoted as "the book of the law." So if the Decalog contains moral law, then the book did too. This shows the utter fallacy of their theory of two laws.

The following passage alone overturns the two-law theory of Adventists: "Master, which is the great commandment in the law? Jesus said unto him, Thou shalt love the Lord thy God with all thy heart, and with all thy soul, and with all thy mind. This is the first and great commandment. And the second is like unto it: Thou shalt love thy neighbor as thyself. On these two commandments hang all the law and the prophets" (Matt. 22:36-40).

1.   These two great commandments were "in the law."

2.   Neither of them is found in the Decalog.

3.   Both of them are in what Adventists call the ceremonial law.

4.   Neither of them was spoken by God, nor written by him, nor engraven on stones, nor put into the ark. Both were given by God to Moses privately, and he wrote them with a pen in the book of the law which was placed in the side of the ark. And yet these two precepts are the greatest of all. Jesus said of the first one that it is "the first of all the commandments." Of the two he said, "There is none other commandments greater than these," and "on these hang all the law." So the greatest commandments are in the book of the law, not on the tables of

stone. This utterly demolishes the Adventist two-law theory. The Ten Commandments on tables of stone, then, were not superior, but inferior, to commandments that were given through Moses in the book of the law.

We shall examine a few more of their contrasts of the two laws as they arrange them.

"1.   Moral: Existed in Eden before the fall. Ceremonial: Was given after the fall."

Answer: Where do they read that the Decalog was given in Eden? Nowhere. This they assume not only without proof, but against the plain record of Exodus 19, 20, and Deuteronomy 5, that it was given at Sinai. So their very first comparison is a failure.

"2.   Moral: Was perfect (Ps. 19:7). Ceremonial: Made nothing perfect (Heb. 7:19)."

This they regard as one of their clearest proofs of the two laws. But where is the proof? Does it follow that if the law is perfect it will or can make sinners perfect? If it could, then, as Paul says, "righteousness should be by the law" (Gal. 3:21). And "then Christ is dead in vain" (Gal. 2:21). The law itself could be perfect, and yet fail to make anybody perfect. However, we believe that Ps. 19:7 is pointing forward to the "truth which came by Christ," the new testament, "the law of Christ." David's Psalms are full of sparkling prophecies of the accomplishments of the gospel. So there is no proof of two laws in the Old Testament, after all.

"3.   Moral: Contains the whole duty of man (Ecci. 12:13). Ceremonial: 'Stood only in meats and drinks, and divers washings, and carnal ordinances' (Heb. 9:10)."

This is fallacious. There is not a particle of evidence that Ecci. 12:13 refers alone to the Decalog. It manifestly embraces all God's commandments on all subjects. There are scores of duties we owe to God and men not even hinted at in the Decalog. Heb. 9:10 refers only to the service of the priests in the temple, which service "stood only in meats and drinks," etc. Here they fail again. Their "two laws" are made out: 1. By pure assumptions. 2. By misapplications of Scripture. 3. By detached phrases here and there taken out of their proper connections. This is "scrapping."

But they assert that such opposite things are said of "the law" that it cannot be the same law all the time. To this we reply: Particular expressions about the law were spoken from widely different standpoints. To apply the Adventists' rule on other Bible subjects would certainly make bad work. Paul said he was "a Jew" (Acts 21:39), and again that he was "a Roman" (Acts 22:25). The Adventist argument for two laws would prove that there were two Pauls. So Christ is "a Lion" and "a Lamb" (Rev. 5:5, 6); "the everlasting Father" (Isa. 9:6), and "born of a woman" (Luke 2:7); "Prince of Life" (Acts 3:15), yet died through weakness (2 Cor. 13:4); "a child" (Isa. 9:6), and yet God (Heb. 1:1-8). Came to bring "peace on earth" (Luke 2:9-14), yet "not peace on earth, but rather division" (Luke 12:51). Two Christs. If Adventist arguments are sound, there must of necessity be two Christs. It would be much harder to reconcile the apparently opposite things said of Christ, than it would be the different things said about the law. There were different sides to Christ's nature, yet he was but one person. So there were different sides to the law, but it was only one law. Viewed in the light of its ultimate design, viz., to prepare the way for Christ, Rom. 10:4; Gal. 3:23-25; in its spirit, Rom. 7:6; in its righteousness, Rom. 8:3, 4— it was "holy and just and good" (Rom. 7:12). But viewed from the side of its mere letter, Rom. 2:29; 7:6; 2 Cor. 3:6, 7; its numerous rites, ceremonies, penalties, and rigorous exactions—it was "the ministration of death" (2 Cor. 3:7), and a "yoke of bondage" (Gal. 5:1-3; Acts 15: 1-10). Yet it was all one law, simply *"the law."*

The book of the law contained the Decalog. The Decalog contained moral precepts and ceremonies. The weekly Sabbath was the chief ceremonial of all the Jewish worship (see chap. 3). The Decalog was partly moral and partly ceremonial. So the book of the law was partly ceremonial, and yet contained scores of moral precepts.

***Proposition 3. The Ten Commandments alone are never called
"the law of the Lord" nor "the law of God."***

Sabbatarians constantly use these two terms, applying them
to the Decalog alone. They are the only ones who keep God's
law, as all others break the Sabbath, the seventh day. But now
notice this fact: The word "law" occurs in the Bible over four
hundred times, yet in not one single instance is the Decalog as a
whole and alone called the law. It is never in a single instance
called "the law of the Lord," or "the law of God." Of course, the
Ten Commandments are a part of the law of God, but only a
part, not the whole. Examine a few texts: Luke 2:22, "The days
of her purification according to the law of Moses"; verse 23, "It
is written in the law of the Lord, Every male that openeth the
womb"; verse 24, it is "said in the law of the Lord, A pair of
turtle doves"; verse 27, "To do for him after the custom of the
law." Here "the law," "the law of the Lord," and "the law of
Moses," all mean the same thing, viz.: the law touching the birth
of a son.

Again, sacrifices, offerings, sabbaths, new moons, and
feasts are all required "in the law of the Lord" (see 2 Cor. 31:3).
Scores of texts like this could be cited, where "the law of the
Lord" includes sacrifices, circumcision, feast-days, and all the
Jewish law. So the law of God is not simply the Decalog, but the
whole law of Moses. In Neh. 8:1, 2, 3, 7, 8, 14, 18, they read "in
the book of the law of Moses," "the law," "the book of the law,"
"in the book of the law of God," "the law which the Lord
commanded by Moses," "the law of God." The law of God, then,
included the whole law of Moses.

No Sabbatarian, therefore, keeps "the law," "the law of
God," or "the law of the Lord"; for if he did he would offer
sacrifices, be circumcised, and live exactly like the Jews. So all
their talk about "keeping the law" amounts to nothing, for none
of them do it. In their attempt to keep a part of that law they
thereby bring themselves under obligations to "keep the whole
law," as Paul argues in Gal. 5:3. But as none of them keep the
whole law, they bring themselves under the curse of the law, by

constantly violating one part while attempting to keep another. This is the very point that Paul made against Judaizing legalists of his day (see Gal. 3:10). The person who keeps one precept of the law just because the *law* says so, thereby acknowledges that the law is binding on him. Then if he neglects some other part of the law, he thereby becomes a transgressor of the very law he professes to keep. This is exactly what Sabbatarians do. They keep the Sabbath because the law says so and thereby become "debtors to do the whole law" (Gal. 5:3). Then they neglect many things in the same law, and so are under the condemnation of the law (Gal. 3:10). But we "are dead to the law," "not under the law," "but under grace"—the New Testament.

Proposition 4. *"The law" was given by Moses and the "law of Moses" includes the Decalog.*

Not that Moses was the author of it, but it was through him God gave it to Israel. This is stated so distinctly and so many times that it is useless to deny it. "The law was given by Moses" (John 1:17). "Did not Moses give you the law?" (John 7:19). "The law which the Lord had commanded by Moses" (Neh. 8:14). *"God's law, which was given by Moses"* (Neh. 10:29). This includes the Decalog. "Moses said, Honor thy father and thy mother" (Mark 7:10). This is the fifth commandment. Again:

"Did not Moses give you the law, and yet none of you keepeth the law? Why go ye about to kill me?" (John 7:19). The law against killing is here called the law of Moses.

In Heb. 10:28 it is said that "he that despised Moses' law died without mercy under two or three witnesses." Persons were put to death for violating the Decalog (see Deut. 17:6). They were put to death for breaking the Sabbath (Exod. 31:14), blasphemy, theft, and the like. Hence the Decalog is included in "the law of Moses."

In Josh. 8:30, 31, we read: "Then Joshua built an altar unto the Lord God of Israel in Mount Ebal, as Moses the servant of the Lord commanded the children of Israel, as it is written in the book of the law of Moses, an altar of whole stones, over which no man hath lift up any iron." It says that this about the altar was written in the "book of the law of Moses." Now turn to Exod. 20:25, the very chapter where the Decalog is found, and there you have the text referred to. This proves beyond denial that the Ten Commandments are in the law of Moses.

Proposition 5. *"The law" was not given till the time of Moses and Sinai.*

The texts quoted prove this. "The law was given by Moses" (John 1:17). "Did not Moses give you the law?" (John 7:19). "For until the law sin was in the world; but sin is not imputed where there is no law. Nevertheless death reigned from Adam to Moses" (Rom. 5:13, 14). The entrance of the law is here located at Moses. Every attempt to place it back of that time contradicts the plain testimony of these texts. The Bible locates the law under the Levitical priesthood. "If therefore perfection were by the Levitical priesthood, for *under it the people received the law"* (Heb. 7:11). This drops the bottom out of Sabbatarianism. So the giving of the law is located "430 years after the covenant with Abraham." "And this I say, that the covenant, that was confirmed before of God in Christ, the law, which was four hundred and thirty years after, cannot disannul" (Gal. 3:17). This brings us to the very year the children of Israel came out of Egypt and arrived at Sinai. "And it came to pass at the end of the four hundred and thirty years, even the self-same day it came to pass, that all the hosts of the Lord went out from the land of Egypt" (Exod. 12:41). Beyond dispute, then, what the Bible calls "the law" was not given till Moses, 2,500 years after Adam, or nearly half the history of the world.

Proposition 6. *Their fathers did not have the Decalog as worded on the tables.*

This Moses directly states. Deut. 4:12, 13 says God spoke to the children of Israel from heaven, and declared to them "his covenant," "even ten commandments." Chapter 5:2, 3 says: "The Lord our God made a covenant with us in Horeb. The Lord *made not this covenant with our fathers,* but with us." Then he repeats the Ten Commandments as that very covenant (vss. 4-22). That their fathers had the law as worded and arranged at Sinai is directly denied by Moses.

Proposition 7. The law was given only to the children of Israel.

This is so manifest in every item of the law that it needs no argument to prove it. Moses says (Deut. 4:8) that no nation has a law so good "as the law which I set before you this day." Then he names the Ten Commandments as a part of it (vss. 10-13). "This is the law which Moses set before the children of Israel" (vs. 44). Then no other nation had the law. This is stated a hundred times over. It was addressed to the Israelites, and to them only.

The very wording of the law proves that it was designed only for them. The Decalog is introduced thus: "I am the Lord thy God, which brought thee out of the land of Egypt, out of the house of bondage" (Exod. 20:2). To whom is that applicable? Only to the Israelite nation. Neither angels, Adam, nor Gentile Christians were ever in Egyptian bondage. Then, the law was not addressed to them. Paul plainly states to whom the law was given. "Who are Israelites; to whom pertaineth the adoption, and the glory, and the covenants, and the giving of the law" (Rom. 9:4). It was given to Israel. In Mal. 4:4 it is clearly stated that the law given in Horeb was "for all Israel."

All these things show that this was a national law worded to fit the condition of the children of Israel at the time.

Proposition 8. The Gentiles did not have the law.

This has been proved already; but Paul directly says so (Rom. 2:14): "For when *the Gentiles, which have not the law,...* these having not the law, are a law unto themselves." This is too plain to need arguing. The Gentiles did not have the law. The law in letter as worded in detail on Sinai was never given to them.

Proposition 9. The rewards and penalties of the law were all temporal.

There are no promises of future rewards, nor threatenings of future punishments, in all the Mosaic law. Every careful student of that law must be aware of this feature of it. The reason is clear. It was a national, temporal law, given for a national, temporal purpose. As a sample of all, see Deut. 28:1-19. If they keep the law, they shall be blessed in children, in goods, in cattle, in health, etc. If they disobey, they shall be cursed in all these. Stoning to death was the penalty for theft, murder, Sabbath-breaking, etc. Hence it was the "ministration of death written and engraven in stones" (2 Cor. 3:7), and "is done away" (vs. 11).

Paul states that the promise of the future inheritance was made to Abraham four hundred and thirty years before the law was given. From this he argues, and forcibly, too, that the keeping of the law was not necessary in order to receive Christ and the inheritance. "Now to Abraham and his seed were the promises made. He saith not, And to seeds, as of many; but as of one, And to thy seed, which is Christ. And this I say, that the covenant, that was confirmed before of God in Christ, the law, which was four hundred and thirty years after, cannot disannul, that it should make the promise of none effect. For if the inheritance be of the law, it is no more of promise: but God gave it to Abraham by promise" (Gal. 3:16-18). "For the promise, that he should be the heir of the world, was not to Abraham, or to his seed, through the 'law, but through the righteousness of faith. For if they which are of the law be heirs, faith is made void, and the promise made of none effect" (Rom. 4:13, 14).

This plainly states that the law was not given with reference to the future inheritance. Surely Abraham did not keep the law, which was not given for several hundred years after he died. But Abraham is the father of the faithful, and not simply of those who were "of the law" (Rom. 4:13-16). This point alone ought to open the eyes of those who contend so earnestly for the keeping of the law as necessary to salvation. We are the children of Abraham (Gal. 3:29) and "walk in the steps of our father Abraham," who was never under the law (see Rom. 4:12-16). We are under the covenant of promise made to Abraham four hundred and thirty years before the law (Gal. 2:15-19; 3:15-19), and not under the covenant of the law from Sinai, which is bondage (Gal. 4:21-31).

Proposition 10. God's eternal law of righteousness existed before the law of Sinai was given.

This proposition is self-evident. Surely God had a law by which to govern his creatures long before Sinai. But "the law," as worded in the Decalog and in the "book of the law," was not given till Moses, 2,500 years after the creation of man. Hence moral obligations did not begin with that law, nor would it cease if that law was abolished. "All unrighteousness is sin" (1 John 5:17); and "sin is the transgression of the law" (1 John 3:4). This text is used by Sabbatarians to prove that every possible sin is always a violation of the Ten Commandments. But, 1. "The law" is the whole Mosaic law, not merely the Decalog. 2. A correct translation entirely spoils this text for them. The word "law" is not in the text in the original. The Revised Version gives it correctly: "Sin is lawlessness." This is the true meaning of the text. Sin is lawlessness, a disregard for some law, but not necessarily the same law.

Adam "sinned" long before that law was given (see Rom. 5:12-14). Cain sinned (Gen. 4:7). The Sodomites were "sinners (Gen. 13:13), and vexed Lot with their unlawful deeds" (2 Pet. 2:8). Surely none of these violated "the law," which was not given till Moses. To say that they must have violated the *principles* of that law is not to the point. When the Jews killed Stephen (Acts 7:59), they violated the principles of the law of Michigan which forbids murder; but did they violate the "law of Michigan"? No; for it was not given for eighteen hundred years after, and they were not under it anyway. So neither Adam, nor the Sodomites could have transgressed the law of Sinai, for it was not yet given. Abraham kept God's laws (Gen. 26:5), but surely not "the law which was four hundred and thirty years after" (Gal. 3:17). All this clearly shows that God had a law before the code of Sinai was given.

Jesus, under the gospel fifteen hundred years later, in

naming the commandments, gives them neither in the same words nor in the same order as found in the Decalog. Further, he mingles them with some precepts from the book of the law as of equal importance with the Ten. Thus: "Do not commit adultery, Do not kill, Do not steal, Do not bear false witness, Defraud not, Honor thy father and mother" (Mark 10:19). This shows that the mere form and order of the commandments is of no consequence as long as the idea is given. The two editions of the Decalog in Exodus 20 and Deuteronomy 5 vary much in the wording; yet one is as good as the other.

In whatever form or manner God chose to communicate his will to men, this would be "his commandments, his statutes, and his laws" (Gen. 26:5). Paul says: "God, who at *sundry times and in divers manners* spake in time past unto the fathers" (Heb. 1:1, 2).

A disregard for his revealed will would be lawlessness— sin. But to claim that God gave the patriarchs his law in the exact form and words of the Ten Commandments is a proofless assumption, contrary to reason and all the clear testimony of Scripture.

Proposition 11. The original law is superior to the law of Sinai.

When asked, "Which is the greatest commandment of the law?" Jesus said: "Thou shalt love the Lord thy God with all thy heart and with all thy soul, and with all thy mind. This is the first and great commandment. And the second is like unto it, Thou shalt love thy neighbor as thyself. On these two commandments hang all the law and the prophets" (Matt. 22:37-40). Neither of these is in the Decalog; but that law hangs on this higher law, and so is inferior to it. These principles, clad in the armor of eternal immutability, lay back of the Mosaic law and existed as they had existed before and exist now.

In its very nature this great law of supreme love to God, and equal love to fellow creatures, must be as eternal and everlasting as God himself. This law governs angels, governed Adam, the patriarchs, the pious Jews while "under the law," and governs Gentile Christians now. It is applicable to all God's creatures in all ages and all worlds. This great law might be worded in different ways at different times and yet the same essential idea be preserved. Thus, Jesus stated the second great commandment in another form: "Therefore all things whatsoever ye would that men should do to you, do ye even so to them; for this is the law and the prophets"(Matt. 7:12). The idea is the same as "thou shalt love thy neighbor as thyself." Evidently this supreme law must have been known to Adam and to the patriarchs, but in just what form we are not told. To say that it was in the exact words of the Decalog is to affirm what can in no wise be proved.

Proposition 12. The Mosaic law was founded upon the higher and original law.

Jesus directly affirms this: "On these two commandments hang all the law." The principles of this great law were interwoven all through the law of Sinai, being the life, "the spirit," or "the righteousness" of "the law" (Rom. 2:26-29; 8:4). As an example, Leviticus 19. Here you have the second great commandment (vs. 18), and the principles of every one of the Ten Commandments. Thus: 1st commandment (vs. 32); 2nd (vs. 4); 3rd (vs. 12); 4th (vs. 30); 5th (vs. 3); 6th (vs. 17); 7th (vs. 29); 8th (vs. 13); 9th (vs. 11); 10th (vs. 35). Mingled among these are commandments about sacrifices (vs. 5); harvest (vs. 9); clothing (vs. 19); priests (vs. 22); first-fruits (vs. 23); wizards (vs. 31); Gentiles (vs. 34), etc. All these are founded upon this higher law and can be changed to fit circumstances without affecting the supreme law, which is ever the same.

Adventists make a great ado over the absurdity of the idea that God should abolish his law at the cross and then immediately reenact nine-tenths of it. They say, "As well cut off your ten fingers to get rid of one bad one, and then stick nine on again." So they go on with a whole jumble of absurdities involved in the position that God's moral law was abolished at the cross and a new one given. But this is only a man of straw of their own making, hence easily demolished. We hold no such absurd position. But the Mosaic law from Sinai was only a national one founded upon the principles of God's moral law.

Even while it existed it did not supersede God's higher law; and when it ended, it in no way affected God's law, which continued right on, unchanged and unchangeable. To illustrate: The State law of Michigan forbids murder, theft, and adultery. In these items it is founded upon God's moral law. Now abolish the law of Michigan. Does that abolish God's law? No. So with the state law of Israel. Neither its enactment on Sinai nor its abolition at the cross in any way changed God's great moral law by which he will judge the world. The Adventist absurdity grows out of their own false theory, that is all. The particular wording of the law as adapted to the Jewish age was "the letter" or "form" of the law for the time being. If a Jew loved God with all his heart, he obediently circumcised his sons, offered burnt sacrifices, paid tithes, kept the Passover, the new moons, the Sabbath, and attended the temple worship, for this was "the law of the Lord" (2 Chron. 31:3; Luke 2:22-27). But if a Christian loves God he will be baptized (Acts 2:38); take the Lord's Supper (1 Cor. 11:24); wash the saints' feet (John 13:1-16; 1 Tim. 5:10); attend meetings (Heb. 10:25); and observe the law of Christ, which is much different from the law the Jews observed. Hence "there is made of necessity a change also of the law" (Heb. 7:12). Those who make the mere letter of the Jewish law an iron rule, and contend for the exact wording under all circumstances and in all ages, miss the spirit of the gospel, and are in bondage to a system out of date (Gal. 3:19-25; 4:21-25; 6:1-3, 14; 2 Cor. 3:3-15).

Proposition 13. The law of Sinai was given to restrain criminals who would obey God only through fear.

Consider this proposition well. A failure to understand this simple fact is the cause of all the blunders Sabbatarians and legalists in their extravagant and unscriptural praises of "the ministration of death, written and engraven in stones" (2 Cor. 3:7). On this point hear Paul state why the law was made and notice that it is of the moral precepts of the law that he speaks. "Knowing this, that the law is not made for a righteous man, but for the lawless and disobedient, for the ungodly and for sinners, for unholy and profane, for murderers of fathers and murderers

of mothers, for man-slayers, for whore-mongers, for them that
defile themselves with mankind, menstealers, for liars, for
perjured persons, and if there be any other thing that is contrary
to sound doctrine" (1 Tim. 1:9, 10). The apostle here refers
directly to the code of Sinai, including the Ten Commandments,
that which prohibited murder, theft, lying, etc. This law, he says,
was not made for a righteous man but for the lawless. Of this law
in another place Paul says: "Wherefore then serveth the law? It
was added because of transgression" (Gal. 3:19). Again, "The
law entered that the offense might abound" (Rom. 5:20), and,
"until the law sin was in the world" (vs. 13). It is manifest that
sin, offense, and transgression existed before "the law" was
given, and that it was given to prohibit already existing crimes.
Evidently God put the race on trial from Adam to Moses under
the same eternal law of right and love to be governed holy men.
But mankind failed shamefully. They did not live by that rule.
They became lawless. Disregard of God and open violence
toward men were increasing till life and property were insecure.
Then God selected one nation, the Hebrews, and gave up the rest
to their own ways (Rom. 1:20-28).

Up to this time God's people had not been a nation by
themselves, but had dwelt among other nations and had been
subject to their civil laws which prohibited or violence and
protected life and property. But as soon they became a nation by
themselves, it became absolutely necessary to have a national
law of their own which would prohibit and punish open crime,
such as murder, theft, adultery, etc. Life and property would not
have been secure without this, because many among them were
wicked lawless men, "stiff-necked and rebellious." If all had
been righteous, if all had loved God and their neighbors, there
would have been no need of a prohibitory law with a death
penalty. We can readily see why Paul says "the law was not
made for a righteous man, but for the lawless. "These lawless
ones would have robbed and murdered the righteous ones had
there been no national, temporal law to protect them; for these
wicked men would have cared little about God's higher law,

which pertains to the future judgment. But as the Jewish government was a theocracy, one in which God himself was ruler, the law required and regulated service to him as well as duties among themselves.

Hence to this nation God gave the law of Sinai (Exod. 20:2). Would it have been given had they obeyed God without it? Paul has settled that point. "The law is not made for a righteous man, but for the lawless" (1 Tim. 1:9). This, then, is not God's original law by which he prefers to govern men. It was a law of prohibitions, threats, pains, and penalties. Its object was to restrain open crime, protect men in their natural rights, and preserve the knowledge of God in the earth till Christ should come (Gal. 3:19-25). In order to keep that nation separate from all others, many burdensome rites were incorporated into the law, which made it a yoke of bondage (Acts 15:10; 5:1-3).

When Christ came, and the Jewish nation was rejected and dispersed, and their national law overthrown, and the gospel went to all nations, that law had served its purpose, and so passed away as a system (Matt. 5:17, 18; Rom. 10:4; Gal. 3:24; Heb. 7:12-19). Now Christians are not under the Aaronic priesthood, nor the Jewish law (Heb. 7:14-19), as was Abraham our father (Gen. 14:18-20), who never had "the law" of Sinai (Gal. 3:17,) but walked by the higher law which governs holy men (Gen. 26:5). The Jewish law being removed, we now come under the same law by which Enoch and Abraham "walked with God."

Now, as in the days before Moses, God's people are not a nation by themselves, but are scattered among all nations, where they are governed and protected by the civil law of those nations. Hence the New Testament provides no civil law for the government of Christians, no temporal penalties for criminals. It would be directly contrary to the nature of the gospel to do either. All this is left to the rulers of nations where Christians happen to be. Criminals are turned over to the magistrates and laws of the land. Paul makes this very plain and puts the question beyond dispute. "Let every soul be subject unto the higher powers. For there is no power but of God: the powers that be are ordained of God. Whosoever therefore resisteth the power, resisteth the ordinance of God; and they that resist shall receive to themselves damnation. For rulers are not a terror to good works, but to the evil. Wilt thou then not be afraid of the power? do that which is good, and thou shalt have praise of the same: for he is the minister of God to thee for good. But if thou do that which is evil, be afraid; for he beareth not the sword in vain: for he is the minister of God, a revenger to execute wrath upon him that doeth evil. Wherefore ye must needs be subject, not only for wrath, but also for conscience sake. For for this cause pay ye tribute also: for they are God's ministers, attending continually upon this very thing" (Rom. 13:1-6).

Here is the prohibitory law for "the lawless." This punishes their crime against society. Their offenses against God's great law will be recompensed at the judgment; but the saints of God must be governed by the higher law, the law of supreme love to God and equal love to fellows. Such obedience can come only from a heart renewed by the Spirit of God (2 Cor. 3:3); and "if ye be led of the Spirit, ye are not under the law" (Gal. 5:18).

Is any man a Christian who refrains from murder, theft, and adultery, simply because the law says "Thou shalt not"? No, indeed; he must refrain from these from a higher motive than that. Then he is governed by a higher law than the Decalog. "Love is the fulfilling of the law" (Rom. 13:10). The dispute concerning the Jewish Sabbath involves this point, the obligation of the letter of the Jewish law.

Proposition 14. *The letter of the law is not binding upon Christians as a coercive code.*

If the letter of the law is binding, then we must be circumcised, offer sacrifices, keep the seventh day, and all the Jewish ritual, for "the law" included the "whole law" (Gal. 3:10; 5:3).

The "righteousness" of the law and the "spirit" of the law is one thing, while "the letter" and outward service is quite another. "Therefore if the uncircumcision keep the righteousness of the law, shall not his uncircumcision be counted for circumcision? And shall not uncircumcision which is by nature, if it fulfil the law, judge thee, who by the letter and circumcision dost transgress the law? For he is not a Jew, which is one outwardly; neither is that circumcision, which is outward in the flesh: but he is a Jew, which is one inwardly; and circumcision is that of the heart, in the spirit, and not in the letter; whose praise is not of men, but of God" (Rom. 2:26-29).

Paul argues that Christians must be circumcised, but not "outwardly in the flesh," as formerly, but "inwardly in the spirit, not in the letter." By this he illustrates the difference between keeping the law now and formerly. So, further on: "Ye are not under the law, but under grace" (Rom. 6:14). In the next chapter he says: "But now we are delivered from the law, that being dead wherein we were held; that we should serve in newness of spirit, and not in the oldness of the letter" (Rom. 7:6).

How can anyone misunderstand language so plain? Now, under Christ, we are delivered from the law; that law is dead, and we serve Christ in the spirit, "not in the old letter." The higher law of God, namely, supreme love to God and equal love to our neighbors, upon which the Jewish law hung, was the "spirit," "righteousness," or real intent of "the law." This "first and great" law Christians do keep, while free from the mere letter of the law, which was bondage.

"For, brethren, ye have been called unto liberty; only use not liberty for an occasion to the flesh, but by love serve one another. For all the law is fulfilled in one word, even in this; Thou shalt love thy neighbor as thyself. But if ye be led of the Spirit, ye are not under the law" (Gal. 5:13, 14, 18). "Not in tables of stone, but in fleshly tables of the heart." "Who also hath made us able ministers of the new testament; not of the letter, but of the spirit: for the letter killeth, but the spirit giveth life" (2 Cor. 3:3, 6). The law for Christians is not that written in the book or on tables of stone—the letter. That which was "written and engraven in stones" is "done away" (vs. 7). It is "that which is abolished" (vs. 13). Christians are under "the law of the Spirit of life"—the new testament.

The Abolition of the Law

Adventists are continually crying, "God's law [meaning the Sinaitic code] is unchangeable." But Paul contradicts them, boldly stating "that there is made of necessity a change also of the law" (Heb. 7:12). "The law was given by Moses, but grace and truth came by Jesus Christ" (John 1:17). "He taketh away the first, that he may establish the second" (Heb. 10:9). Two laws could not stand in the same dispensation. Therefore to establish the gospel—grace and truth, which came by Christ—the law was "taken away." The manner in which it was taken away is thus explained in Christ's own words: "Think not that I am come to destroy the law, or the prophets: I am not come to destroy, but to fulfill. For verily I say unto you, Till heaven and earth pass, one jot or one tittle shall in no wise pass from the law, till all be fulfilled" (Matt. 5:17, 18). This text clearly states that when the law reaches its fulfillment it will pass away. It will not pass till fulfilled. So it is not eternal, but when fulfilled it was to reach an end. Then, the Lord points to himself as the fulfillment of the law and prophets—"For Christ is the end of the law" (Rom. 10:4). "The law was our schoolmaster to bring us unto Christ" (Gal. 3:24). Since Christ is come "we are no longer under a schoolmaster" (vs. 25) "not under the law, but under grace" (Rom. 6:14). This nails the matter fast, and utterly refutes the Adventist plea for the perpetuity of the law.

Sabbatarians argue that as long as heaven and earth last the law will continue. Their own argument proves that the law is not eternal; for Jesus said, "Heaven and earth shall pass away" (Luke 21:33). But Jesus did not say that the law would continue till heaven and earth had passed away. The idea is that heaven and earth would sooner pass away than one letter of the law fail in being fulfilled. "It is easier for heaven and earth to pass, than one tittle of the law to fail" (Luke 16:17). That is the idea. Not the length of time the law was to continue, but the certainty that it would not fail to be fulfilled. Christ said it would continue till fulfilled. This proves that it would be fulfilled and pass away some time. But when is the time? Christ plainly says, 'I am come to fulfill it.' Hence Paul rightly concludes that "Christ is *the end* of the law." *"Fulfill:* To complete; to fill up."—*Webster.* "To bring to a close, end, finish, complete."—*Greenfield.* Then, the law ended with Christ. "Heaven and earth shall sooner perish than one iota or one tittle of the law shall perish without attaining to its end."—*Macknight, Camrpbell, Doddridge.* Exactly. Christ says he came to fulfill the law. Did he? Hear him after his resurrection: "These are the words which I spake unto you, while I was yet with you, *that all things must be fulfilled,* which were written in the law of Moses, and in the prophets, and in the Psalms, concerning me" (Luke 24:44). "And when they had fulfilled all that was written of him, they took him down from the tree" (Acts 13:29). The law was fulfilled and ended at the cross. Was "nailed to the cross" (Col. 2:14-16).

Adventists make a tremendous blunder when they confine "the law" in Matt. 5:17, 18 to the Decalog. "The law" includes all the law of Moses. The "law and the prophets" is a term that applies to the entire Old Testament. All commentaries agree on this. But the Scriptural proof is abundant. "Witnessed by the law and the prophets" (Rom. 3:21). "The reading of the law and the prophets" (Acts 13:15). "This is the law and the prophets" (Matt. 7:12). *"All the prophets* and the law" (Matt. 11:13). "All the law and the prophets" (Matt. 22:40). "They have Moses and the prophets....If they hear not Moses and the prophets" (Luke 16:29, 31). "Written in the law of Moses, and in the prophets...concerning me" (Luke 24:44). "Written in the law and in the prophets" (Acts 24:14). "Him, of whom Moses in the law, and the prophets, did write" (John 1:45). "Moses and the prophets" and "the law and the prophets" are the same thing. "The law" is defined as "Moses," "the law of Moses." And "the law and the prophets" reach their fulfillment in Christ. This is the whole Old Testament. The Adventist argument on Matt. 5:17, 18 will make circumcision and all Moses' law binding to all time and eternity.

This law was a "shadow" of Christ's atonement and redemptive blessings (Heb. 10:1-3). Its sacrifices, blood, Passover, sin-offerings, altars, etc., all pointed to him. Its sanctuary pointed forward to his greater house; the church; its Sabbath to the sweet soul-rest he gives. When Christ the substance came to earth, the shadow—law—vanished away.

"The law and the prophets were until John" (Luke 16:16). His ministry was "the beginning of the gospel" (Mark 1:1-3). When the law reached its fulfillment in Christ, it was not necessary to destroy it. Therefore he says, "I am not come to destroy, but to fulfill." To illustrate this point. Suppose that the legislature of Pennsylvania had passed a law forbidding the killing of any game in the State for a period of ten years, and that this law had come into force January 1, 1919. On January 1, 1929, that law would die of itself, and sportsmen would not wait for the legislature to pass an act to abolish or destroy that law. Its very construction and wording would teach all intelligent men that it could not continue in force longer than January 1, 1929. Just so it was with the law. "It was added because of transgressions, *till the seed should come*" (Gal. 3:19). "To thy seed, which is Christ" (vs. 16). This so clearly teaches that the law was but a temporary institution, to continue in force only until the promised seed—Christ—should come, that there is no appeal from it. The coming of Christ—his death—is the date, then, when the law expired. There was no necessity to destroy it in order to make it null and void; for its limit ended when it was fulfilled in Christ, and of necessity it became dead. This shows the utter fallacy of the Seventh-day Adventists' position. Christ fulfilled the law, and it passed away after having served its purpose.

"Having abolished in his flesh the enmity, even the law of commandments contained in ordinances" (Eph. 2:15). The law was a partition wall between the Jews and the Gentiles. Christ broke down this wall, by abolishing *"the law of command-ments,"* around which clustered all the ordinances and ceremonies of the Old Testament. This was done "that he might reconcile both unto God in one body by the cross, having slain the enmity thereby" (vs. 16). The date of the abolition of the law is placed at the cross. "Blotting out the handwriting of ordinances that was against us, which was contrary to us, and took it out of the way, nailing it to his cross; and having spoiled principalities and powers, he made a shew of them openly, triumphing over them in it. Let no man therefore judge you in meat, or of the new moon, or of the sabbath days" (Col. 2:14-16). That which was nailed to the cross included the Sabbath. The whole system ended at the cross. Since that, "if ye be led of the Spirit, ye are not under the law" (Gal. 5:18). "Christ is become of no effect unto you, whosoever of you are justified by the law; ye are fallen from grace" (vs. 4). This applies forcibly to all Saturday-keepers.

"Know ye not, brethren, (for I speak to them that know the law,) how that the law hath dominion over a man as long as he liveth? For the woman which hath an husband is bound by the law to her husband so long as he liveth; but if the husband be dead, she is loosed from the law of her husband. So then if, while her husband liveth, she be married to another man, she shall be called an adulteress: but if her husband be dead, she is free from that law; so that she is no adulteress, though she be married to another man. Wherefore, my brethren, ye also are become dead to the law by the body of Christ; that ye should be married to another, even to him who is raised from the dead, that we should bring forth fruit unto God. But now we are delivered from the law, that being dead wherein we were held; that we should serve in newness of spirit, and not in the oldness of the letter" (Rom. 7:1-4, 6). Here is a plain lesson. Who can misunderstand it? Paul uses the law of matrimony to teach the abolition of the Mosaic system. That first husband was "the law"; the wife was the church—Israel. But the first husband died; viz., the law was abolished. It was "nailed to the cross," then buried. In recent years the Sabbatarians hunted its grave, and dug it up. All they found was the skeleton. This they stood up, but it fell down. So they have invented many props by which they expect to keep it standing. But by the eternal truth their props must fall and their idolized, decayed system of abolished "shadows"— the law—be buried in the same grave in which Jesus laid it nineteen hundred years ago.

Ye are become "dead to the law," and are now married to Christ. He is the second husband. Sabbatarians are married to the law, while ours is alive forevermore. They cling to a ghostly shadow, while we enjoy the substance. They are under the "ministration of death," while we cling to the "law of life." They wear the "yoke of bondage," while we rejoice in the "law of liberty." Their glory is "done away," while ours "remains." While Moses is read "the vail is on their hearts," but with us this vail is "done away in Christ." They cling to the law, while we cleave to the gospel. They grope in the smoke of Sinai, while we stand in the light of Zion. O Adventist friend, forsake your system, and accept the truth, which will make you free.

Moses, the Mediator of the Law

"Mediate. — To interpose; to intercede." — *Webster.* Then, a mediator is one who interposes or mediates between parties, one who stands in the middle between two. *Mesites* is the Greek. It is defined in *Young's Concordance,* "middleman, mediator." "A go-between, one who intervenes between two parties. It is applied to Moses as an interpreter or mere medium of communication between Jehovah and the Israelites (Gal. 3:19, 20). Jesus Christ is…'the mediator of the new covenant' (Heb. 12:24; 8:6), or 'of the new testament' (Heb. *9:15)."—Smith and Barnum.*

The law "was ordained by angels in the hand of a mediator" (Gal. 3:19). We have but to inquire, Who was the middleman at the giving of the law? Moses himself answers: "The Lord made a covenant with us in Horeb….The Lord talked with you face to face in the mount out of the midst of the fire, (*I stood between the Lord and you at that time,* to show you the word of the Lord)" (Deut. 5:2-7). Moses, then, filled the exact office of a mediator.

"Jesus Christ never claimed to be the mediator in the giving of the law on Sinai, but he acknowledged Moses as filling that office. Of the many instances we shall cite only a few. 'Did not Moses give you the law, and yet none of you keepeth the law? Why go ye about to kill me?' (John 7:19). 'For the law was given by Moses, but grace and truth came by Jesus Christ' (John 1:17). 'For Moses said, Honor thy father and thy mother; and, Whoso curseth father or mother, let him die the death' (Mark 7:10). In this last instance Jesus quotes one precept from the Decalog (see Exod. 20:12) and Deut. 5:16, and one from the judgments that God gave Israel through Moses immediately following the Ten Statutes (see Exod. 21:17). This proves that Moses was the mediator of the whole book of the law, Ten Commandments and all. And the same laws ascribed to Moses in Mark 7:10 are ascribed to God in Matt. 17:4, showing, as many other similar passages do, that the whole law system was the law of God, its author, and yet the law of Moses, its mediator, or medium of communication. There is therefore no distinction between the law of God and the law of Moses, as the Adventists teach.

"To say that John 1:17 relates only to the ceremonial part of the law is utterly ridiculous. It betrays a false creed that forces the mind out of the channels of good common sense. In the passage the covenants of the two great dispensations are referred to. 'The law was given by Moses'—he was the mediator of that economy. 'But grace and truth [the new testament] came by Jesus Christ,' who is now the mediator of the same. It may seem strange that we should spend a moment to show a fact so obvious. But in the name of Jesus we must do the duty of a watchman, and warn the people against the dark pitfall of legalism.

"'The law was until John'; that is, he was the first herald of the new dispensation. His preaching and baptism are denominated 'the beginning of the gospel of Jesus Christ, the Son of God'(Mark 1:1-4).

"Though there were precious promises of Christ mingled in

the book of the law, and there is a perfect law found in the gospel, the two dispensations are separate and distinct. Their distinguishing characteristics are frequently compared, as 'law' and 'gospel,' or 'law' and 'truth.' Christ never said he was the mediator of the former system. But, saith he, 'Did not Moses give you the law?' Do you ask what law? The whole law covenant, of course. That he included the Decalog in the 'law' which he said Moses gave the Jews, is evident. For he adds, 'None of you keep the law. Why go ye about to kill me?' They purposed in their hearts to violate the law of Moses by killing him, which they also did, even that law which said, 'Thou shalt not kill.'

"'But,' say our Sabbatarian friends, 'There is but one mediator, the man Christ Jesus.' Certainly there was but one under the law, and there is but one now. Moses and Christ did not both officiate in the same dispensation. Christ succeeded Moses, and the new testament superseded the old.

"Again they say, 'A mediator is a savior and Moses could not save.' The idea of a savior from sin is not in the word 'mediator.' But Moses was a deliverer of the Israelites out of bondage, which is even called a 'redemption.' Hence he was a glorious figure of Jesus Christ, our Redeemer.

'But,' said the debater, 'if Moses was the mediator between God and Israel, what did they do for a mediator after his death? Answer: His mediation consisted chiefly in giving them the law and leading them out of Egypt, and wherein the law system needed further mediation, Jesus said, 'The scribes and the Pharisees sit in Moses' seat' (Matt. 23:2). Their business was to teach and enforce the law.

"One more prop we remove. 'At least Moses was not a mediator in giving the Ten Commandments; for God spoke them aloud in the ears of all the people, and then wrote them himself on the tables of stone.' To this let Moses answer. 'I stood between the Lord and you at that time, to show you the word of the Lord: for ye were afraid by reason of the fire, and went not up into the mount.'

"'Moses gave you the law,' i. e., 'thou shalt not kill.' Moses said, Honor thy father,' etc., the fifth commandment.

"'The law was ordained in the hands of a mediator.' In whose hands were placed the tables of stone? And Moses turned and went down from the mount, and the two tables of the testimony were in his hands (Exod. 32:15). 'And it came to pass, when Moses came down from Mount Sinai with the two tables of the testimony in Moses' hand' (Exod. 34:29).

"A few texts will establish the fact that 'the law of Moses,' also called 'the law of God,' is the entire law of that dispensation. In Neh. 8:1 we read that the people 'spake unto Ezra the scribe to bring the book of the law of Moses, which the Lord had commanded to Israel.' It was brought. 'So they read in the book, in the law of God.' So the law of Moses and the law of God are the same book (vs. 8). And in Neh. 10:29, we are told the people entered 'into an oath, to walk in God's law, which was given by Moses the servant of God, and to observe and do all the commandments of the Lord, our Lord.' Here the law-teacher is utterly confounded. The law of Moses and the law of God are one and the same. It is called 'God's law which was given by Moses,' and the same one law includes 'all the commandments of the Lord, our Lord.'

'Be ye therefore very courageous to keep and to do all that is written in the book of the law of Moses, that ye turn not aside therefrom to the right hand or to the left; that ye come not among these nations, these that remain among you; neither make mention of the name of their gods, nor cause to swear by them, neither serve them, nor bow yourselves unto them' (Josh. 23:6, 7). The entire law system is called the 'law of Moses,' and in obeying it they were not even to mention the name of the gods of the heathen, neither swear by them, nor serve them. Here we see the law of Moses covered the first commandment.

'And keep the charge of the Lord thy God, to walk in his ways, to keep his statutes, and his commandments, and his judgments, and his testimonies, as it is written in the law of Moses, that thou mayest prosper in all that thou doest, and

hithersoever thou turnest thyself' (1 Kings 2:3). These words
utterly demolish the Adventist theory. 'The charge of the Lord
thy God,' 'his ways,' 'his statutes,' 'his testimonies,' were all
'written in the law of Moses.' What, then, we should like to
know, was left to constitute 'the law of God,' which the vain
imaginations of Saturday-keepers distinguish from 'the law of
Moses,' and which they say has survived the abolition? Were not
the Ten Precepts God's commandments? Then, they were
'written in the law of Moses.' Were they statutes? There they are
written. 'And his testimonies, were written in the law of Moses.'
What is meant by these? The Ten Commandments. Proof, read
Exod. 25:16; 31:18; 32:15; 34:29; 40:20. Here are five clear
statements that the testimonies were the ten laws on the tables of
stone. To these may be added many passages which call the
place of their deposit 'the ark of the testimonies,' all of which
prove the same thing. How perfectly these scriptures sweep away
the refuge of lies that the Ten Commandments are distinct, from
the law of Moses, and remain still in force since the law of
Moses is abolished!

'Neither will I anymore remove the foot of Israel from out
of the land which I have appointed for your fathers; so that they
will take heed to do all that I have commanded them, according
to the *whole law* and the statutes and the ordinances by the hand
of Moses' (2 Chron. 33:8). Can a man be honest before God and
hold the Sabbatarian view after reading such scriptures? All that
God commanded them, even 'the *whole law* and the statutes are
the ordinances,' was given by the hand of Moses. This proves
that Moses was the mediator spoken of in Gal. 3:11 and it also
proves that there were not two laws, but one law. Every duty
enjoined by Jehovah upon the nation was by the hand of Moses.

'"Thou camest down also upon Mount Sinai, and spakest with
them from heaven, and gavest them right judgments, and true
laws, good statutes and commandments: and madest known unto
them thy holy sabbath and commandedest them precepts,
statutes, and laws, by the hand of Moses thy servant' (Neh. 9:13,
14). Here again all the laws, statutes, and commandments that

God gave the people on Mount Sinai. including the Sabbath were given by the hand of Moses, and is Moses' law as well as God's law. This scripture proves that the Sabbath was there given by God, and not before; that Moses was mediator in its ministration; and that all the law forms one system.

"'These are the testimonies, and the statutes, and the judgments, which Moses spake unto the children of Israel after they came forth out of Egypt' (Deut. 4:45). 'The testimonies,' we have seen, were those upon the stone tables, and though God spoke them to all Israel, and Moses wrote them in the book, he is represented as having spoke them to the children of Israel, because he was the mediator of the whole law economy. The same are called 'the commandments of the Lord our God, his testimonies, an his statutes' in Deut. 6:17.

"So it is positively false that the law is divided into two laws. It is all the law of God, and all the law of Moses But why multiply texts? Surely the foregoing are sufficient to prove these things. And yet upon the contrary theory hangs the Adventist creed. They know very well that the New Testament, in the most positive terms, asserts the abrogation of the old covenant, called 'the law'; and indeed they are forced to admit the fact. Therefore there is no possible chance to maintain their Saturday-keeping. But if that entire code passed away, what now remains? We answer, Just what the inspired apostle says remains. 'The new testament,' 'the law of Christ.'— *The Sabbath.*

The Decalog

The Seventh-day Adventists point the people to the Decalog as God's eternal law, superior to all else, that which governs angels in heaven governed Adam in Eden, and will govern the teeming millions of redeemed ones to all eternity. These extravagant claims are the main pillars underneath the whole doctrine and argument used by them for the observance of the seventh day. If Adventists are wrong here, their whole doctrine falls to the ground. And fall it must under the hammer of eternal truth.

When the lawyer asked Jesus, "Which is the great

commandment in the law?" Jesus did not point to the Decalog. In fact, he did not quote one precept from the tables of stone. "Jesus said unto him, Thou shalt love the Lord thy God with all thy heart, and with all thy soul, and with all thy mind. This is the first and great commandment. And the second is like unto it, Thou shalt love thy neighbor as thyself. On these two commandments hang all the law and the prophets" (Matt. 22:37-40). Here are two commands not found in the Decalog. Yet the Master said that these are "the first of all the commandments," and that "there is none other commandment greater than these" (Mark 12:29-31). This spoils the Adventist theory in pointing to the Decalog as God's superior and eternal law. These two—enjoining love to God and fellow beings—are *first* and *greatest.* On them the Decalog hangs. Hence it is inferior to that higher law which is eternal. The Decalog was hung to that first and greater law. But twenty-five hundred years of man's history passed before this took place. "The law was given by Moses." Not until Moses' time was the Decalog given and coupled to that higher law. This is settled beyond question by Moses himself. Referring directly to the Ten Commandments (see Deut. 5:2-22), he says, "The Lord made not this covenant with our fathers, but with us, even us [Israel" (vs. 3).

The very wording of the Decalog proves that it was given to Israel as a nation alone. On the tables were written all the words God spoke in the mount (Deut. 9:10). These words you will find written out in full in Deut. 5:6-22. "These words" "he wrote in two tables of stone" (vs. 22). Now lay down the book and carefully read verses 6 to 22 inclusive, and you have exactly what was on the tables—the Decalog. To whom does it apply? To whom it was given is told by the very first words: "I am the Lord thy God, which brought thee out of the land of Egypt, from the house of bondage. Thou shalt have none other gods before me," etc. (Exod. 20:2, 3; Deut. 5:6, 7). This was on the tables, written with God's own finger, and placed in the ark. When Adventist lecturers hang up their charts, it will be noticed that they have left out this part, and begun with "Thou shalt have no other gods." Why do they do this? The reason is apparent. To put the whole Decalog on their chart would betray the falsity of their claims. Was Egypt the abode of Adam? How many of the millions of Christians which constitute the new testament church were under King Pharaoh in Egyptian bondage? Not one. It cannot possibly apply to any but the Israelitish nation.

Look at the Sabbath commandment as written on the stone tables. "Keep the Sabbath Day to sanctify it, as the Lord thy God hath commanded thee. Six days thou shalt labor, and do all thy work: but the seventh day is the Sabbath of the Lord thy God: in it thou shalt not do any work, thou, nor thy son, nor thy daughter, nor thy man servant, nor thy maid servant, nor thine ox, nor thine ass, nor any of thy cattle, nor thy stranger that is within thy gates; that thy man servant and thy maid servant may rest as well as thou. And remember that thou wast a servant in the land of Egypt, and that the Lord thy God brought thee out thence through a mighty hand and by a stretched out arm: therefore the Lord thy God commanded thee to keep the Sabbath Day" (Deut. 5:12-15). Can this apply to all people in all ages? Can it apply to angels? Will it apply to the redeemed in heaven forever? Reason and common sense answer, "No." Angels—servants in the land of Egypt! "Thine ox, nor thine ass, nor any of thy cattle." Do the angels in heaven own oxen, work asses, and feed cattle? Will this be true of the redeemed millions around the throne in eternity? "Thy man servant, nor thy maid servant, nor thy stranger that is within thy gates." Would this apply to Adam in Eden? Did he have servants, and let strangers in his gates back there? The language shows that Israel is referred to. It cannot possibly apply elsewhere. "Thy stranger in thy gates" refers to the Gentiles that entered the gates of their cities.

"Honor thy father and thy mother: that thy days may be long upon the land which the Lord thy God giveth thee." What land was given? Answer: Canaan. To whom was it given? Answer: Israel. Then the fifth commandment was given to Israel. Angels do not have fathers and mothers. How can they honor what they do not have? Are the angels under the fifth commandment? Preposterous. Then that law cannot govern the hosts of heaven. It was given to a single nation—Israel—in a limited territory—Canaan.

"Thou shalt not commit adultery." Does this command govern angels in heaven? Will it be the law that will rule the untold millions of immortal beings around the throne in eternity? These lecturers hang up their charts, and teach men that this law is eternal, governs angels, and will govern the redeemed forever; that it must stand eternally. This is all done to save their idolized Sabbath. But their argument is false from the ground up. The Decalog cannot apply universally. It was given by Moses from God to Israel to restrain wickedness from men's hearts. Think of God telling the angels, who are spirit-beings, "Thou shalt not commit adultery." Would that not sound a little strange to the millions in heaven with immortal, spiritual and glorified bodies? Yet on just such absurdities rests the whole structure of Sabbatarianism.

"Thou shalt not covet thy neighbor's wife." Strange language this would have been to Adam while in Eden. Stranger yet it would sound to angels in heaven, and to the immortal saints around the throne, where "they neither marry, nor are given in marriage."

The wording of the Decalog throughout shows that it was only a prohibitory national law, worded to fit the circumstances, and adapted to the social condition of the Jews as a nation in the land of Canaan. To apply it to Eden, to angels, and to heaven, is nonsense.

Adventists make a great ado over the fact that the Ten Commandments were spoken by God's voice, written by his finger, engraven in stones, and placed in the ark. "Why," ask they, "was it thus kept separate, if not more prominent than the rest of the law?" We answer: The Ten Commandments were written by Moses in the book of the law, along with the other precepts (see Exodus 20 and Deuteronomy 5). They were included in the book of the covenant which was sprinkled with blood, and which Paul says "was taken away" and "abolished" that Christ might establish the "second" or "new covenant."

But it was customary at the time of the giving of the law, that, when a solemn covenant or agreement was entered into between parties, some object be selected as a witness or testimony of the transaction. I shall cite a few examples. Jacob set up a pillar as a witness of his vow to God (see Gen. 2:18). When Jacob and Laban made a covenant, "they took stones and made a heap." "And Laban said, This heap is a witness between me and thee this day" (Gen. 31:45-48). On this point I quote from Canright:

"Just so when the solemn covenant was made between God and Israel at Sinai, the Lord gave them the tables of stone to be always kept as a witness or 'testimony' of that agreement. Hence they are called 'the tables of testimony,' that is, witness (Exod. 31:18). So the tabernacle was 'the tabernacle of testimony' (Num. 1:53), or, 'the tabernacle of witness' (Num. 17:7; Acts 7:44). These tables of stone, then, containing some of the chief items of the law, were always to be kept as *'witness'* of the covenant which Israel had made to keep that law. This is the reason why the Decalog was given as it was, and not because it was a perfect and eternal law in and of itself." This is sound and logical. These reasons are so simple and clear that the imaginary reasonings invented by Sabbatarians fade away.

Another thought just here: The Decalog of necessity was only a national law for Israel and temporal in its obligations, because the penalty for its violation was stoning to death. "He that despised Moses' law died without mercy under two or three witnesses" (Heb. 10:28). Adventists admit that the penalty of the law was abolished at the cross, and this admission proves that the law itself ceased there too; for a law without a penalty is a nullity.

But as a last effort, these preachers cry, "If the Decalog is no longer in force, then there is nothing to condemn crime, such as adultery, idolatry, etc." This is another man of straw that the fire of truth will consume. The New Testament does condemn these.

Idolatry—"*Little* children, keep yourselves from idols" (1 John 5:21). "Neither be ye idolaters" (1 Cor. 10:7). "Wherefore, my dearly beloved, flee from idolatry" (1 Cor. 10:14).

Adultery—"*Know* ye not that the unrighteous shall not inherit the kingdom of God? Be not deceived: neither fornicators, nor idolaters, nor adulterers, nor effeminate, nor abusers of themselves with mankind, nor thieves, nor covetous, nor drunkards, nor revilers, nor extortioners, shall inherit the kingdom of God" (1 Cor. 6:9, 10).

Theft—"*Steal* no more" (Eph. 4:28).

Lying—"*Lie* not one to another" (Col. 3:9). "All liars shall have their portion in the lake which burneth with fire and brimstone" (Rev. 21:8).

Murder—"*No* murderer hath eternal life abiding in him" (1 John 3:15).

Covetousness—"*Covetousness,* let it not once be named among you" (Eph. 5:3). "Covetousness, which is idolatry" (Col. 3:5).

The New Testament forbids not only evils condemned in the Decalog, but also scores of others not mentioned in that code, such as drunkenness, love of pleasure, pride, anger, impatience, selfishness, boasting, filthy talk, evil thoughts, foolishness, uncleanness, strife, hatred, envyings, revelings, etc. Thus, it became necessary to supersede the Decalog and all that clustered around it with the new testament, which is "a better covenant, established upon better promises."

The Seventh-Day Sabbath as Mentioned in the New Testament

Since the "first" or "old" covenant—the law—that enjoined the observance of the seventh day, was abolished and ended at the cross, and the "new" and "better" covenant has taken its place, what do we find in the New Testament? Not one command to keep the Sabbath of the former covenant. Not one threat against anyone for working on that day. While over and over long lists of sins are mentioned, covering every kind of disobedience, not once is Sabbath-breaking mentioned. In Paul's fourteen Epistles he names the Sabbath but once, and then shows that it was abolished and nailed to the cross (Col. 2:14-17). In the Epistles of James, Peter, John, and Jude, the word "sabbath" cannot be found. Compare this with Adventist literature, and note the contrast. They talk and write more on the Sabbath than on any other theme. It is the life of their system. The fourth commandment of the "ministration of death" can nowhere be found in the New Testament. We are not Jews nor Adventists, but New Testament Christians, under the truth that came by Jesus Christ; and since there is not one command in the new covenant, which is our rule of faith, to keep the seventh day, we are under no obligations to do so. To find such command, people must go back to the law; and to observe it because Moses' law enjoined it is to put our necks into "the yoke of bondage," to become "children of the bondwoman" (Gal. 4:21-30); but we who are called into the liberties of the gospel "are not children of the bondwoman, but of the free" (vs. 31).

One Adventist minister in our presence, when nettled by our positive demand for one command in the New Testament for the observance of the seventh day, lit upon Matt. 24:20, and said the language was equivalent to a command. This shows the desperate straits to which these people are driven. 'Pray ye that your flight be not in the winter, neither on the Sabbath Day." On this text we shall remark: 1. The subject was not the observance of the day. Jesus was speaking of the destruction of Jerusalem, and the safety of the Christians in fleeing out of the doomed city. In the winter the roads would be bad, so that their flight would be much retarded. On the Jewish Sabbath all the gates of the cities were closed and locked (see Adam Clarke or any other reliable authority), and hence escape would be impossible. That is all there is to the text. 2. Simply fleeing out of a city or country would not desecrate the day, as Adventists themselves admit. Then, there is no proof nor command in the text for the observance of the day. The Lord was simply providing for the safety of the Christians.

But it is argued that Jesus kept the day, and that

consequently we too must keep it. This is a very weak argument. Jesus was born under the law (Gal. 4:4), and lived under it until its abolition at the cross (Col. 2:14). He evidently kept it in the main—the whole law. He was circumcised. Does that bind circumcision on us? He kept the Passover (Luke 22:7-15). Do Sabbatarians keep it because Jesus did? Never. He sent a man to offer a gift according to the law (Matt. 8:4), and commanded his disciples to do all that the scribes taught (Matt. 23:2, 3). Are these things obligatory upon us now? Adventists themselves admit that they are not. This shows the fallacy of their argument for Sabbath-keeping. While Jesus lived as a Jew under the Jewish law, he kept that law—circumcision, Passover, Sabbath, and all. But it ended at the cross (Col. 2:14).

But the women kept the Sabbath "according to the commandments" (Luke 23:56). This is considered strong proof by Sabbatarians. But where is the argument? The women rested while Jesus was in the grave and dead. He had not risen. Many things concerning the law and its abrogation were yet mystified to them. Christ promised that when the Holy Ghost should come, he would teach them many things, and open their understanding. The fact that certain Jewish women rested on that day is no more proof that the Jewish Sabbath is binding on Gentile Christians than the facts that even after the day of Pentecost many thousands of believing Jews were "zealous for the law" and that Paul circumcised Timothy (Acts 21:20; 16:3) or that circumcision is binding on us today.

Every mention of the Sabbath in the Book of Acts is in connection with Jewish worship. The Jews kept their Sabbath, and assembled on that day. Paul, as his custom was, availed himself of this opportunity to preach the gospel to them, and so reasoned with them on the Sabbath-days. Had he gone to the Jewish synagogue on any other day, he would have found no congregation to address. "Wherever the apostles entered the Jewish synagogue on the Sabbath to preach, it was before the Christian church was planted in such places." And even could it be proved that for a time the Jewish Christians met from custom on the Sabbath for worship, that would not bind Sabbath-keeping on Gentile Christians; for the Jews that believed, circumcised and kept all the rest of the law for a time (Acts 21:20, 21). But at the council held at Jerusalem in A. D. 46, as recorded in Acts 15, it was decided not to bind the law on the Gentile churches. Here again there is no proof in favor of Saturday-keeping.

With great demonstration it is argued that the term "sabbath" occurs in the New Testament fifty-nine times, and always refers to the seventh day, and that hence the seventh day must be the New-Testament Sabbath. But the same argument would bring all the ceremonies of Moses' law under the gospel. Let us test their reasoning. The Passover is mentioned in the New Testament twenty-eight times, and always refers to the feast kept by the Jews; therefore that feast must be a New-Testament ordinance. Circumcision is found fifty-nine times in the New Testament; hence, according to Adventist argument, it must still be in vogue. Such reasoning betrays weakness. That the feasts, sacrifices, Passover, sabbaths, circumcision, etc., of Moses' law are frequently mentioned in the New Testament, is no proof that they are still obligatory upon the people of God.

The Old Sabbath Repealed[3]

By reading Rom. 2:12, 14-16, it is seen that there are two kinds of precepts: those that exist in man's consciousness, independent of law to enforce them, and those duties that are wholly created by the code that enjoins them. The former are commanded because they are inherent principles of right; the latter are right only because they are commanded. The former are unchangeable; the latter rest wholly on the will of the lawgiver, and may be changed whenever his wisdom dictates. The law stamped by the Creator upon our inner being is that which Paul says we "establish by faith." Therefore, with the exception of the few positive monumental ordinances of the new testament, it is simply the reimpress of that holy law of our being which was

---

[3] This chapter is take from *The Sabbath* by D. S. Warner.

stamped upon us by the Creator, and which was partly obscured by sin, but is fully restored to the soul in entire sanctification (Heb. 10:14, 15), while the written New Testament is an expression of the same perfect law. The passage in Rom. 13:9 asserts that there is nothing of the law system carried over into the new covenant but that which love itself dictates, that which existed as a principle of right back of all outward legislation. Now the question to be settled and upon which the perpetuity of the seventh day Sabbath depends is this: Was this institution written in man's inward conscience? or was it wholly the product of positive legislation? If the former, it remains unchangeable; if the latter, it has passed away. We shall now prove that that seventh-day Sabbath was created wholly by legislation; belonged to the monumental and shadowy rites of the Jew's religion; was for a temporary purpose, and was therefore repealable, and actually was abolished.

First, we prove that its object was to serve as a sign between God and the Israelite nation. "And the Lord spake unto Moses, saying, Speak thou also unto the children of Israel, saying, Verily my sabbaths ye shall keep: for it is a sign between me and you throughout your generations; that ye may know that I am the Lord that doth sanctify you. Ye shall keep the Sabbath therefore; for it is holy unto you: every one that defileth it shall surely be put to death: for whosoever doeth any work therein, that soul shall be cut off from among his people. Six days may work be done; but in the seventh is the Sabbath of rest, holy to the Lord: whosoever doeth any work in the Sabbath Day, he shall surely be put to death. Wherefore the children of Israel shall keep the Sabbath to observe the Sabbath throughout their generations, for a perpetual covenant. *It is a sign between me and the children of Israel* forever" (Exod. 31:12-17).

Here we are twice told that the Sabbath of the law was a sign between God and the Jewish nation throughout their generations. It is strictly confined to them, and there is not a word indicating that God would ever make it anything else than a national statute in Israel. It was a sign of the redemption of that nation from Egyptian bondage; for that deliverance is called a redemption in Exod. 15:12, 13. We have positive proof that the Sabbath was instituted to commemorate that event. After the repetition of the command to keep the seventh day, thus we read: "And remember that thou wast a servant in the land of Egypt, and that the Lord thy God brought thee out thence through a mighty hand and by a stretched out arm: *therefore the Lord thy God commanded thee to keep the Sabbath Day"* (Deut. 5:15). Can anything be plainer? The Sabbath was given as a remembrancer to the Jews, a monument of their bondage in a strange land and their deliverance therefrom. To deny this is to dispute the Bible. But if that be the object of that rest-day, no one else has anything to do with it, nor it with them. In Neh. 9:9-14 this redemption out of the land of bondage, and the Sabbath, as a sign and monument of the same, are again seen coupled together.

Now let us show you a parallel sign, or monument of the same redemption from bondage. "Unleavened bread shall be eaten seven days; and there shall no leavened bread be seen with thee, neither shall there be leaven seen with thee in all thy quarters. And thou shalt show thy son in that day, saying, This is done because of that which the Lord did unto me when I came forth out of Egypt. And it shall be for a sign unto thee upon thine hand, and for a memorial between thine eyes, that the Lord's law may be in thy mouth for with a strong hand hath the Lord brought thee out of Egypt" (Exod. 13:7-9). The Passover was instituted for a "sign," a "memorial" of the deliverance of Israel out of Egypt. And we have seen that the Sabbath was given expressly for the same object and to the same people, throughout their generations. If, therefore, the Passover feast belonged only to the Jewish rites, so did the Sabbath. If the Passover feast is abolished—and no Adventist denies it—so is its like sign, the Jewish Sabbath. These conclusions cannot be gainsaid.

That the Sabbath was a sign of redemption out of Egypt we again prove, by Ezek. 20:10, 12, as follows: "Wherefore I caused them to go forth out of the land of Egypt, and brought them into the wilderness." "Moreover also I gave them my sabbaths to be a sign between me and them, that they might know that I am the Lord that sanctify them." Here we have again the redemption out of Egypt followed by the Sabbath as a sign or monument of that deliverance. "A sign between me and them, that they might know that I am the Lord that sanctify them;" namely, separated them from the heathen among whom they were in bondage. How could that Sabbath have been designed for all nations, which was given expressly as a sign or mark of separation of the Jews from all other nations? In fact, it could not be universal and at the same time the peculiar badge of one nation. We leave it classified just where the Bible places it—among the signs and rites of the Jews, and as such it has passed away.

But says the Saturday-keeper, "That Sabbath must yet be in force; because God said, 'The children of Israel shall keep the Sabbath, to observe the Sabbath throughout their generations for a perpetual covenant,' and 'It is a sign between me and the children of Israel forever' (Exod. 31:16, 17)." While the word "forever," speaking of spiritual things and of future destinies, etc., means unending, it is also used in speaking of laws to indicate that they are in continuous force, standing, permanent. In such case it indicates a law unchangeable and unrepealable while the system of which it is a part lasts. This we shall now prove by the Bible. When the Passover was first instituted in Egypt, God said, "Ye shall observe this thing for an ordinance to thee and to thy sons forever" (Exod. 12:24). After giving directions for the use of olive-oil in the lamps of the tabernacle, he said. "It shall be a statute forever unto their generation" (Exod. 27:21). Following directions for the high-priestly garments that Aaron and his sons were to wear in their ministration, it is written "It shall be a statute forever unto him and his seed after him" (Exod. 28:43). And the same thing is affirmed of nearly every ceremonial precept of the law. So, then, the Sabbath was to be a "sign forever" just as the Passover and other types and shadows were. They have passed away long ago; so also has that Sabbath. The Bible leaves no peg upon which to hang its perpetuity.

As we have proved that both the Passover and the law Sabbath were signs and memorials of the deliverance of the children of Israel out of Egypt and from the slaying angel, we shall now prove that the Sabbath as well as the Passover was a type and shadow of things to come in the dispensation of Christ. That the Passover pointed back to Egypt, and also cast its shadow forward to Christ upon the cross, all see and admit. So was the Sabbath a sign of things past and things to come. The very fact that it commemorated the exodus from Egypt makes it a type of our redemption for that deliverance sustains a typical relation to our salvation from the bondage of sin.

"And you, being dead in your sins and the uncircumcision of your flesh, hath he quickened together with him, having forgiven you all trespasses; blotting out the handwriting of ordinances that was against us, which was contrary to us, and took it out of the way, nailing it to his cross" (Col. 2:13, 14). The law, with all its ordinances and shadowing rites, expired with Christ upon the cross. 'Let no man therefore judge you in meat, or in drink, or in respect of an holy day, or of the new moon, or of the sabbath-days: which are a shadow of things to come; but the body of Christ" (Col. 2:16, 17). Let no man judge you by the laws of that code which had served its time and purpose, and vanished away. The laws respecting meats are no longer to be bound upon our consciences, neither "holy day," law feast-days, etc., nor yet monthly feasts determined by the moon; yea, and let no man judge you of the "sabbath-days." These "sabbath-days" cannot be specially referred to annual or monthly sabbaths, for such are included in the former specifications. They must, therefore, have special reference to the round of weekly Sabbaths. They are all nailed to the cross and taken away.

The Sabbath was a "shadow of things to come, but the body is of Christ"; that is, it had typical reference to things "of Christ." So we see that the Sabbath was an exact parallel of the Passover. Both were signs between God and the Jews; both were memorials of the deliverance out of Egypt; both pointed forward to Christ; and both have met their antitype and passed away. The Passover foreshadowed the offering of the body of Christ upon the cross. Of what was the Sabbath a shadow? Its distinguishing feature was rest, absolute cessation from labor. And just as certainly as "Christ our Passover is sacrificed for us," Christ is our rest. Hear his gracious words: "Come unto me, all ye that labor and are heavy-laden, and I will give you rest...And ye shall find rest unto your souls" (Matt. 11:28, 29). This beautiful rest in Christ will be more fully considered further on. There is scarcely an important item in the entire law system that does not shadow some fact in the plan of salvation.

Just as all works were peremptorily excluded on that Sabbath, so must men utterly cease from their own works in taking Christ our rest. The law said, "Do no work, but rest and live." The gospel says, "Believe in God, without bringing a single meritorious work, and in Christ you shall find rest, and your soul shall live." And even more certain than the penalty of death for Sabbath work is death to the soul that would seek or maintain justification before God on the ground of good works.

Yes, "the sabbath-days: which are a shadow of things to come; but the body [the substance] is of Christ." This inspired testimony is true. The Sabbath was a striking shadow of a condition in our salvation, and, with all other types and shadows, passed away when the type met its antitype—when Christ our salvation appeared.

Under this head, "The Old Sabbath Repealed," we now, with the weapons of truth, attack and demolish one of the strongholds of the law-wrangling sect; namely, the relation of the Sabbath to creation. "It is a sign between me and the children of Israel forever: for in six days the Lord made heaven and earth, and on the seventh day he rested, and was refreshed" (Exod. 31:17). Along with the other memorial and typical elements of the Sabbatic institution, it was commemorative of the work of creation. Upon this fact Adventists base an argument that it was universal, for all mankind. But we accept the uniform statements of Jehovah that he gave that Sabbath law exclusively to the

Israelites through their generations, as an all-sufficient refutation of this argument.

Again, Adventists tell us that the Sabbath's being commemorative of creation proves it unchangeable. They quote Alexander Campbell as saying that before God could change the day of the Sabbath he would have to make a new creation. Such talk is very natural, and doubtless very plausible with the wisdom of this world; but to the spiritual it only betrays spiritual ignorance. Salvation would reveal to such reasoners that a "new creation" has indeed taken place. Accordingly, we read, "The first man Adam was made a quickening spirit" (1 Côr. 15:45).

Two Adams suggest a new creation. The first man Adam was the head of the original creation of God; but falling into sin, his race became disqualified for the lofty end of their existence. But in due time appears another, an "heavenly" Adam, a "quickening spirit," the life-giving power of God. He defeats Satan and sin, and works a new creation. As the first Adam stands at the head of the spoiled creation, so the second Adam heads a new creation. All in this new creation are of heavenly character.

How did we come into the creation headed by the first Adam? By natural birth. How do we enter the new and heavenly race? By being "born again." "Marvel not that I said unto thee, Ye must be born again." This was an incomprehensible mystery to Nicodemus, and it is not better known by the earthly today. The natural man receiveth not the things of the Spirit of God, neither can he know them." John testifies that "as many as received him [Jesus] ""were born...of God" (John 1:12, 13). "Being born again" is the testimony of 1 Pet. 1:23. John gives us the heavenly character of all who are thus inducted into the new creation. "Whosoever is born of God doth not commit sin; for his seed remaineth in him: and he cannot sin, because he is born of God" (1 John 3:9). Lest some might conclude that John had drawn the standard too high, he repeats with an emphasized assurance, "We know that whosoever is born of God sinneth not; but he that is begotten of God keepeth himself, and the wicked one toucheth him not" (1 John 5:18).

Comparing their own lives with this standard, the Adventists, Russellites, and other modern legalists found themselves far beneath it. Therefore they have concluded and do teach that only spiritual conception takes place, and that in the resurrection, or in some other event of the future, the birth will take place. This is another new doctrine of devils. Both John and Peter in the passages quoted above testify that the birth has taken place in all who believe in Christ.

"Of his own will begat he us with the word of truth, that we should be a kind of first-fruits of his creatures" (Jas. 1:18). The apostles, having been begotten of God, were a kind of first-fruits of his creatures—first in the new creation. "Therefore if any man be in Christ, he is a new creature:...And all things are of God" (2 Cor. 5:17, 18). Five different translations render, "If anyone is in Christ, he is a *new creation.*" "So that if any one be in Christ there is a *new creation.*"

A wonderful fact. As God created the physical world himself, without the aid of creatures, so, we are told, in "the new creation" "all things are of God." "For we are his workmanship, created in Christ Jesus unto good works" (Eph. 2:10). God first created man in his own image; and "the new man, which is after God [after the pattern of his moral image] is [again] created in righteousness and true holiness" (Eph. 4:24). In Col. 3:10 we are plainly told that the new creation restores the soul to the image of the Creator. "For in Christ Jesus neither circumcision availeth anything, nor uncircumcision but a new creature" (Gal. 6:15). By seven translations it is very properly translated, *"A new creation."*

In many places redemption is compared to the creation. Take, for instance, the creation of light. "For God, who commanded the light to shine out of darkness, hath shined in our hearts, to give the light of the knowledge of the glory of God in the face of Jesus Christ" (2 Cor. 4:6).

They who are of the first Adam are earthly; they of the second Adam are heavenly. The law, including the seventh day, was not given for the righteous, but for the ungodly, the earthly. Will God translate us from the earthly into the heavenly and yet leave us under the Sabbath that was made for the earthly? How utterly ridiculous the idea that the second Adam should come into this sin-lost world, start a new creation, and leave us under a Sabbath that identifies us with the fallen Adam and the world that lieth in iniquity!

Behold the striking analogy. When God completed the work of creation, "he rested from his labors, and was refreshed." And twenty-five hundred years later, when he saw fit to command a day of utter abstinence from labor, he chose that day which commemorated the finishing of creation, so that in its observance the children of Israel not only commemorated the miraculous hand of God which had brought them out of Egypt, but also kept before their eyes the fact that God is the Creator of all things. Such a remembrancer was needed by a people only born after the flesh, and who were soon to enter a land flooded with gross idolatry, where God was not known as the Creator. But how ridiculous the idea that redeemed and illuminated Christians, who know God, even the one true and living God, need a Sabbath to keep them from deifying some other object besides the Creator.

The seventh-day Sabbath, therefore, embodied no element that made it unchangeable and unrepealable. It was a positive statute, created wholly by the decree of the divine Law-giver, and was therefore subject to removal by his decree. when. with the rest of the code in which it was embodied, it had served its time and object, and when God moved forward in the order of his plan, and the new dispensation and creation sprang forth. It was a sign that God had sanctified Israel, that is, separated them from the heathen nations. It was a sign or memorial of that nation's deliverance out of Egypt, and it passed away when that nation forfeited their place as the chosen people of God, soon to be dispersed again among all nations. It was a shadow of things to come and was nailed to the cross with all the other shadows and types. It was a part of the covenant written on stone; and the

New Testament teaches in the most positive manner, and by a large number of passages, that that covenant was abolished; that Christ himself, the mediator of the new testament, took away the first that he might establish the second. Therefore it not only was repealable, but actually was repealed by authority of Him who has all power in heaven and earth; and in so doing he showed that he is "lord of the Sabbath also."

And should any law-teacher attempt to argue that the Sabbath of the Jews survived that Sinaitic law because it was introduced before the general giving of the law, as seen in Exodus 16, we answer, So was the Passover instituted prior to the ministration of the law on Sinai, even before Israel came out of Egypt (Exodus 12), and yet it passed away with the death of the first covenant and its shadows. It and its sister "sign," the Sabbath, were both incorporated in the law system given on Sinai, and both passed away with it. The old Sabbath, then, is dead and gone. And is there any occasion for mourning over its decease? Have we lost anything in the death and decay of the old covenant, since Christ is the "mediator of a better covenant, established upon better promises"? Is there anything mournful in the death of that "wherein we [the Jews] were held," since we are married to Christ?

Those desiring to be teachers of the law now tell us that "we are not under the law, only in the sense that we obey the law, and therefore do not come under its condemnations." How directly this conflicts with the Word of God. It teaches that we are "not under the law," and are "delivered from the law," just as a woman is no longer under the obligations of the marriage covenant after her husband is dead. The law that bound her in obedience has passed away. "She is freed from that law." His lips are silent. He issues no commands; she obeys none from him. Thus, by the plain illustration God teaches us that the converted Jew is not under the law, nor under obligations to obey it.

The Jewish Sabbath Abolished

"Blotting out the handwriting of ordinances that was against us, which was contrary to us, and took it out of the way, nailing it to his cross....Let no man therefore judge you in meat, or in drink, or in respect of an holy day, or of the new moon, or of the sabbath-days; which are a shadow of things to come; but the body is of Christ" (Col. 2:14-17). Here is a clear, positive statement that the Sabbath was taken out of the way by nailing it to the cross, and therefore no one has a right to judge us for its non-observance. This single declaration of Paul's refutes all the theories of Sabbatarians. There it stands and mocks all their efforts. All kinds of twists and turns have been made to explain away its meaning, but it defies their doctrines. The Sabbath was nailed to the cross. When "that which was written and engraven in stones" was "done away" and "abolished," as Paul declares in 2 Corinthians 3, the Sabbath went with it; for it lay in the very heart of the Sinaitic covenant, which "vanished away" (Heb. 8:13).

The law was but a shadow (Heb. 10:1), and Paul classes the Sabbath as one of those shadows that have passed away. An attempt is made to identify the "sabbath-days" of Col. 2:16 with the feast-days and holy days of the law, monthly and yearly. This is a poor argument. Paul includes all the holy days of the Jews in the "meats" and "drinks," "holy days," and "new moons"; so there is nothing left for the "sabbath-days" but the weekly Sabbath. The word "sabbath" is found in the New Testament sixty times. Adventists themselves admit that fiftynine times it means the weekly Sabbath, but in the sixtieth case, where the very same word is found in both the Greek and the English, they say it means something else. Isn't that strange? "The sabbath" means the seventh day fifty-nine times, but the sixtieth time it does not! Preposterous! When "the sabbath," or "the sabbath-days," in fifty-nine places in the New Testament refers to the weekly rest-day, it does in the sixtieth place.

But it is objected that "sabbath-days" in Col. 2:16 is a plural term, and that hence it cannot refer to the weekly rest-day. This reasoning is so flimsy that Sabbatarians ought to be ashamed of it. The Sabbath is frequently in Scripture spoken of in the plural.

This is true both in the Old and the New Testament. "My sabbaths ye shall keep" (Exod. 31:13). "Keep my sabbaths" (Lev. 19:3, 30). "Eunuchs that keep my sabbaths" (Isa. 56:4). "Mock at her sabbaths" (Lam. 1:7). "I gave them my sabbaths" (Ezek. 20:12). "Polluted my sabbaths" (vs. 16). "Three *sabbath-days* reasoned with them" (Acts 17:2). "Is it lawful to heal on the *sabbath-days?*" (Matt. 12:10). "On the *sabbath-days* the priests in the temple profane the Sabbath" (vs. 5). "Taught them on the *sabbath-days*" (Luke 4:31). "Let no one therefore judge you…in respect of the *sabbath-days*" (Col. 2:16). Same thing exactly. Anyone can see at a glance that the "sabbaths" and the "sabbath-days" in all these texts refer to the weekly rest-day; and these very sabbath-days, Paul says, were "nailed to the cross."

Another point worthy of note is this: The same Greek word and the same form of the word that Paul uses in Col. 2:16, is used elsewhere for the weekly sabbath. Thus: "Gathered sticks upon the Sabbath Day " (Num. 15:32). "In the end of the Sabbath " (Matt. 28:1). "On the Sabbath Day " (Acts 13:14; Luke 4:16). I shall now quote from the Decalog: "Keep the Sabbath day" (Deut. 5:12). "Remember the Sabbath Day to keep it holy" (Exod. 20:8). "Let no man therefore judge you…in respect of the sabbath-days " (Col. 2:16). The Sabbath in Col. 2:16 can refer only to the Sabbath of the Decalog. "The only word ever used in the Bible for the weekly Sabbath is the very one Paul did use in Col. 2:16." So the weekly sabbath-days have passed away.

That the sabbath-days referred to by Paul in Col. 2:16 have direct reference to the weekly round of rest-days is beyond doubt when we remember that he is simply quoting from the Old Testament—the law and the prophets—where the same list is several times mentioned, and in every instance includes the seventh day. In Numbers 28th and 29th chapters we have a full account of all offerings to be made on the different days of the year. The daily offerings are mentioned in the 28th chapter, verses 3-8; the weekly offerings, verses 9, 10. "And on the sabbath-day two lambs," etc. "This is the burnt offering of every sabbath." Next the new moon, or monthly, offerings. "And in the beginning of your months ye shall offer a burnt offering unto the Lord" (vss. 11-15). Next came the yearly or annual feast-days, extending from 28:16 to 29:39. These were their "set feasts" (vs. 39). Here we have the list complete—daily, weekly, monthly, and yearly.

"Behold, I build an house to the name of the Lord my God, to dedicate it to him, and to burn before him sweet incense, and for the continual shewbread, and for the burnt offerings morning and evening, on the sabbaths, and on the new moons, and on the solemn feasts of the Lord our God. This is an ordinance forever to Israel" (2 Chron. 2:4).

"He appointed also the king's portion of his substance for the burnt offerings, to wit, for the morning and evening burnt offerings, and the burnt offerings for the Sabbaths, and for the new moons, and for the set feasts, as it is written in the law of the Lord" (2 Chron. 31:3).

"Even after a certain rate every day, offering according to the commandment of Moses on the Sabbaths, and on the new moons, and on the solemn feasts, three times in the year, even in the feast of unleavened bread, and in the feast of weeks, and in the feast of tabernacles" (2 Chron. 8:13).

"And to stand every morning to thank and praise the Lord, and likewise at even; and to offer all burnt sacrifices unto the Lord in the Sabbaths, in the new moons, and on the set feasts, by number, according to the order commanded unto them, continually before the Lord" (1 Chron. 23:30, 31).

"And it shall be the prince's part to give burnt offerings, and meat-offerings, and drink-offerings, in the feasts, and in the new moons, and in the Sabbaths, in all solemnities of the house of Israel: he shall prepare the sin-offering, and the meat-offering, and the burnt offering, and the peace-offerings, to make reconciliation for the house of Israel" (Ezek. 45:17).

"For the shewbread, and for the continual meat-offering, and for the continual burnt offering, of the Sabbaths, of the new moons, for the set feasts, and for the holy things, and for the sin-offerings to make an atonement for Israel, and for all the work of the house of our God" (Neh. 10:33).

All these texts are given to show that over and over the identical list Paul uses in Col. 2:16 is used in the law, and in every case the weekly Sabbath is referred to. Time and again we have the *yearly* feast-days or holy days *'monthly* or new moons, and *weekly* Sabbaths all classified as Paul does.

Now since these days are abolished "nailed to the cross," and we have come to the substance—Christ; since we have obtained that which these things foreshadowed—to go back to those law days and their observance is hateful to God. "Bring no more vain oblations, incense is an abomination unto me; the new moons and Sabbaths, the calling of assemblies, I cannot away with; it is iniquity, even the solemn meeting. Your new moons and your appointed feasts my soul hateth: they are a trouble unto me; I am weary to bear them" (Isa. 1:13, 14).

By going back under the "yoke of bondage" and to the observance of the Jewish Sabbath, Sabbatarians are doing the very things which are hateful to God. They cling to a ghostly "shadow," while we enjoy the substance. No wonder Paul said to those Galatians that "desired to be under the law," and, like modern Sabbatarians, had become "bewitched," "Ye observe days [sabbath-days—weekly], and months [new moons], and times [yearly feasts], and years [sabbatical years]. *I am afraid of you"* (Gal. 4:10, 11). Here is the identical list that Paul says was nailed to the cross and therefore are no longer to be observed. By going back to their observance, people fall from grace and become enslaved "to weak and beggarly elements" (Gal. 4:9-11; 5:1-8; 4:21-31).

The New Covenant

"Behold, I make all things new." This is the message of the gospel. Christ came to inaugurate a new creation, an entire new order of things. The seers of old foretold and anxiously looked for the dawning of a better day, a day of salvation, a day when the kingdom of heaven would be established upon earth. The law, its offerings, sacrifices, blood, tabernacle, altars, priesthood, feasts, Sabbath, etc., were but types, figures, and shadows of the glories of this new and better day. We now have a new dispensation, "new testament," "new covenant," "new Jerusalem," new church, new kingdom, "new creation," "new man," "new heart," "new-born babes," "new commandments" (1 John 13:34; 1 John 2:8); "new name," "new and living way," "walk in newness of life," and "serve in newness of spirit." "Old things are passed away; behold *all things* are become new" (2 Cor. 5:17).

In this new dispensation we cannot go back to the Sabbath of the old. The Sabbath enjoined in the first covenant passed away when Christ came and made "all things new." So it was prophesied, "Behold, the days come, saith the Lord, that I will make a new covenant with the house of Israel, and with the house of Judah: not according to the covenant that I made with their fathers in the day that I took them by the hand to bring them out of the land of Egypt" (Jer. 31:31, 32). This new covenant is not according to the one made with Israel when God led them out of Egypt. The covenant God made with them at that time was placed in the ark. "The ark, wherein is the covenant of the Lord, which he made with our fathers, when he brought them out of the land of Egypt" (1 Kings 8:21). And "there was nothing in the ark save the two tables of stone" (vs. 9). So that which was written on the tables of stone—the Ten Commandments—was the covenant made at that time. But this new one that Jeremiah declared the Lord would make was not to be according to the one written in stones. It is "a better covenant, which was established upon better promises" (Heb. 8:6). "By so much was Jesus made a surety of a better testament" (Heb. 7:22). This new covenant is the "new testament" (Heb. 9:15). The two covenants are termed "first" and "second" (Heb. 8:7). When Christ delivered the new he took away the first. "He taketh away the first, that he may establish the second" (Heb. 10:9). "In that he saith, A new covenant, he hath made the first old. Now that which decayeth and waxeth old is ready to vanish away" (Heb. 8:13). We are

Christians under the new testament, and not Jews under the old. The first, with its Sabbath, temple, blood, oblations, etc., has vanished away, while the new is the "everlasting covenant" (Heb. 13:20).

The Law of Christ

"For the law was given by Moses, but grace and truth came by Jesus Christ" (John 1:17). "Jesus the mediator of the new covenant testament, margin " (Heb. 12:24). "Bear ye one another's burdens, and so fulfill the law of Christ" (Gal. 6:2). Here are contrasted the two systems. The first was "the law" given by Moses, its mediator; the second is "grace and truth," the new testament, which came by Christ, its mediator. The new testament is "the law of Christ." This is the law Christians are now under.

In Isa. 42:1-7 we have a clear prediction of the coming of Christ and his redemptive work. "And the isles shall wait for his law" (vs. 4). The law of Moses was given to one nation—Israel. But of the law of Christ—the new testament—it was foretold that "the isles" should wait for it. "The isles" here mean the different nations of earth. The gospel is for all people and nations. The command is, "Preach the gospel to every creature" (Mark 16:15), "Teach all nations" (Matt. 28:19). The gospel is "his [Christ's] law." The isles and the ends of the earth waited for this law; it is the standard of judgment in the earth.

Christ is the "one lawgiver" of this dispensation (Jas. 4:12). For God at "sundry times and in divers various manners" spake unto the fathers in time past, but "hath in these last days spoken unto us by his Son" (Heb. 1:1, 2). In the presence of Moses on the mount, God said of Christ, "This is my beloved Son; *hear ye him*" (Matt. 17:1-5). Moses and his law are ruled out of this dispensation, and Christ and his superior law now rule in its stead. To go back to Moses is to reject Christ. To go under the law is to ignore the gospel.

Christ taught the people "as one having authority" (Matt. 7:29). The precepts he taught are his law. We are under the "law of Christ" (1 Cor. 9:21). "Under Christ's *law.*"—*Emphatic Diaglott.* His law is the truth (John 1:17). The law of Moses gendered to bondage (Gal. 4:24), while the truth makes men free (John 8:32). We obey and walk in the truth (3 John 3). The law of Christ is the standard of conviction to sinners. When guilty souls fall at the mercy-seat for pardon, the law of Sinai never enters their minds. They consider only how they have grieved the Spirit of Christ, and broken his law—the new testament.

The new testament is a much higher law than the old. It not only condemns all manner of sin, but lifts up a standard of holy living far above the stone-table law. The grandest lessons of moral and religious truth ever spoken to men were given in Christ's Sermon on the Mount. The New Testament condemns sin in every form, lifts up the standard of righteousness and holiness in life and experience, and offers life and salvation to all. It is "the perfect law of liberty" (Jas. 1:25), "the law of the Spirit of life in Christ Jesus" (Rom. 8:2). To break Moses' law— the Sabbath, etc.—was to be stoned to death. The penalty was temporal. But to break Christ's law is to be worthy of eternal damnation. In the day of judgment the Decalog will not be our standard of judgment, hut "the word that I Christ have spoken, the same shall judge him at the last day" (John 12:48). "When the Lord Jesus shall be revealed from heaven with his mighty angels, in flaming fire taking vengeance on them that know not God," punishment will not be meted out to those who disregard the letter of the law as written in the tables of stone, but punishment will then be given to those "that obey not the gospel of our Lord Jesus Christ" (2 Thess. 1:7-9). The law of Christ— the gospel—will be the standard by which we shall be judged in that day. To disobey the precepts of Christ is to sin. And to sin against his law is to make ourselves liable to eternal judgment and punishment. Obedience to Christ is what the New Testament enjoins (2 Cor. 10:5; Heb. 5:9). But not once in all the New Testament—the law of Christ, that law by which we shall be judged in the last day—are we commanded to keep the seventh-day Sabbath. We can observe every precept of the law of liberty, stand clear in his sight, and yet never observe the seventh day, which was one of the shadows of the law dispensation.

The Christian's Law

Sabbatarians are constantly crying, "We must keep God's commandments." This is true. But where they err is in applying the term "commandments" exclusively to the ten written on stone. They quote such texts as 1 John 3:22; 2:4; Rev. 12:17; 22:14, and apply them to the old stone-table law. But they assume the very thing that they cannot prove. Do these texts show that the word "commandments" refers to the Ten Commandments? Not at all. Such a position is entirely errone-ous. More than eight hundred times we have the term "commandments" in the Bible. After a careful examination, I find that it means more than the Ten in about ninety-eight texts out of one hundred. In the former dispensation it was a general term for all the requirements of Moses' law. If Adventists mean to keep the commandments of the law, they will have to keep all the precepts of Moses; for there were many other precepts enjoined that were as much the commandments of God as the Ten. Circumcision, sacrifices, and all are summed up time and again and called "the commandments." Jesus quoted two as the greatest "commandments of the law," and neither is in the Decalog (Matt. 22:35-40).

But since the law dispensation has been superseded by the gospel, the precepts of Christ and his inspired apostles are the commandments of God that are binding upon Christians. The commandments referred to in the different Epistles and Revelation are not the ones on tables of stone, which Paul declares are abolished, but are the requirements of the new testament. For three and one-half years Jesus preached "the gospel of the kingdom of God" to this world. This was afterwards written and handed to us by inspired apostles. That gospel, which is the law of Christ, contains scores of precepts and commandments. They are the commandments of God, for he spoke them by his Son (Heb. 1:1, 2). The Father gave Christ commandment what to say (John 12:49), and he spoke this to mankind. Therefore the precepts of the new testament are "the commandments of God and the testimony of Jesus Christ." How dark and godless the leaven of Adventism, which prevents people from seeing any precepts binding as commandments other than those which were spoken on Sinai. Surely the vail is on their hearts.

Jesus taught men to repent, believe the gospel, forgive their fellow men, resist evil, love their enemies, be perfect, sin no more, pray in secret, be baptized, wash one another's feet, observe the communion supper, and scores of other things. These are his commandments. Now, he says: "If ye love me, keep *my* commandments" (John 14:15). "He that hath *my* commandments, and keepeth them, he it is that loveth me" (vs. 21). "If a man love me, he will keep *my words*" (vs. 23). "He that loveth me not keepeth not my sayings" (vs. 24). "Ye are my friends, *if ye do whatsoever I command you*" (John 15:14). The "words" or "sayings" of Jesus are his commandments. To be a commandment-keeper in this dispensation is to obey the sayings of Jesus. But where did Jesus ever command us to keep the seventh day? Nowhere. In his last commission Christ enjoined upon us to teach the people "to observe all things whatsoever I have commanded you" (Matt. 28:20). If we obey that commission we shall never teach men to observe the seventh-day Sabbath; for in all the four Gospels there is no record that Christ ever commanded its observance. I emphasize: *Not once* did Christ command the observance of the seventh day.

Paul says, "If a man think himself to be a prophet, or spiritual, let him acknowledge that the things that I write unto you are the commandments of the Lord" (1 Cor. 14:37). Then, the teachings of Paul are the commandments of the Lord. All true "prophets" (ministers) and "spiritual" people acknowledge this. If the Adventists would admit this point, they would at once see what are the commandments now in force. All the teachings of Paul are "the commandments of the Lord." Where, I ask, in all Paul's Epistles does he command us to keep the seventh-day

Sabbath? Nowhere. The only place where he mentions it by name is Col. 2:14-16, and there he teaches that it was "nailed to the cross." In Gal. 4:9-11 he reproved those who went back to its observance. The commandments of the Lord that Christians keep say not a word about sabbath-days.

Again, says the apostle, "For I have received of the Lord that which also I delivered unto you" (1 Cor. 11:23), and I have "kept back nothing that was profitable unto you" (Acts 20:20). Where in all Paul's ministry, as recorded in the Acts and in his Epistles, did he deliver to the churches any instructions to keep the seventh day? Nowhere. Not a single sentence or text can we find. Yet he kept back "nothing that was profitable." "And ye know what commandments we gave you by the Lord Jesus" (1 Thess. 4:2). "The commandments of us the apostles of the Lord and Savior" (2 Pet. 3:2). All the precepts of the New Testament, then, are the commandments of the Lord that are binding upon Christians to observe. We are commandment-keepers when we observe these. But since there is not a single command in the new covenant to keep the seventh day as a Sabbath, we are under no obligation to do so.

The Gospel Rest

"Sabbath" means "rest." Sabbatarians admit this. Hear Uriah Smith (leading Adventist), "The word 'sabbath' means 'rest.' That is the one sole idea it conveys, first, last, and all the way between."—*What Was Nailed to the Cross*, page 11. Granted. Now we have but to inquire what the rest of God's people in the new covenant consists of, and we have the Sabbath of this dispensation. Here is the answer:

"Let us therefore fear, lest, a promise being left us of entering into his rest, any of you should seem to come short of it. For unto us was the gospel preached, as well as unto them: but the word preached did not profit them, not being mixed with faith in them that heard it. For we which have believed do enter into rest, as he said, As I have sworn in my wrath, if they shall enter into my rest: although the works were finished from the foundation of the world. For he spake in a certain place of the seventh day on this wise, And God did rest the seventh day from all his works. And in this place again, If they shall enter into my rest. Seeing therefore it remaineth that some must enter therein, and they to whom it was first preached entered not in because of unbelief: again, he limiteth a certam day, saying in David, Today, after so long a time, as it is said, Today if ye will hear his voice, harden not your hearts. For if Jesus [Joshua, margin] had given them rest, then would he not afterwards have spoken of another day. There remaineth therefore a rest to the people of God. For he that is entered into his rest, he also hath ceased from his own works, as God did from his. Let us labor therefore to enter into that rest, lest any man fall after the same example of unbelief" (Heb. 4:1-11).

The whole Epistle to the Hebrews is a powerful treatise on the high and lofty privileges extended to God's people through Christ's atonement. Christian perfection is a golden thread that runs from one end to the other. Into this deeper, richer, sweeter experience to be found "within the vail," in the "holiest of all," the Hebrews are urged by the blood of Jesus "to enter." This happy state enjoyed by those who are sanctified the writer calls "rest." He urged the Hebrew brethren "to enter that rest." Nor is this rest deferred till a future millennium; but "we which have believed *do enter* into rest." A present experience. This is denominated "his Christ's rest," "my rest." A rest we find in Jesus Christ. We inquire, What is it? The answer is clear: "Come unto me, all ye that labor and are heavy-laden, and I will give you rest. And ye shall find rest *unto your souls*" (Matt. 11:28, 29). The Sabbath rest of the gospel is a rest of the soul. This rest we find in the bosom of his love. "I will give you rest." Oh, how sweet! He who calmed the raging storm, and said, "Peace be still," speaks to the storm-tossed soul on the mad billows of sin, saying, "I will give you rest." This blessed rest is found in Christ's redeeming love. It is enjoyed in perfect holiness. It is a rest that gives "quietness and assurance forever." Isaiah speaks of it thus: "And in that day there shall be a root of Jesse, which shall stand for an ensign of the people; to it shall the Gentiles seek: and his rest shall be glorious" (Isa. 11:10). A glorious rest. "Ye shall find rest for your souls" (Jer. 6:16). And this sweet tranquil rest we that have believed "do enter." It is the Sabbath of the new covenant.

This spiritual Sabbath rest was never fully realized under the law. The seers of old prophesied concerning it, but never possessed it. "If Jesus [Joshua] had given them rest, then would he not afterward have spoken of another day." The law day was one of types and shadows. So God "limited a certain day," "another day," wherein he would give the people rest in Christ. The writer to the Hebrews plainly tells us that it is *"today"*—this gospel day of salvation. In this day all the shadows of the law reach the substance in Christ.

In Hebrews 4, reference is made to both the old and the new sabbaths, and that with which the former stood in typical relation. In verse 4 the seventh day is mentioned as a rest, and then immediately the writer conveys the mind of the reader to the spiritual rest that "we which have believed do enter." "If they shall enter into my rest." He shows clearly that the seventh day was a type of the Christian's rest which is entered by faith, and that this glorious soul-rest is our Sabbath. "There remaineth therefore a rest to the people of God" (vs. 9). "There remaineth therefore a Sabbath rest for the people of God."—*A. Layman and Revised Version.* "There is then a Sabbath rest left for the people of God."—*Thomas.* "There remains a Sabbatism to the people of God."—*Interlinear.*

Of this higher and better Sabbath the seventh day was a shadow. "The sabbath-days: which are a shadow of things to come; but the body is of Christ" (Col. 2:16, 17). The law Sabbath was a shadow of something that we were to receive in Christ. The thing that we receive in him is a "glorious" "rest unto our souls." We enter it by faith. "We which have believed do enter into rest." This spiritual rest is denominated a "Sabbath rest" that "remains for the people of God." This is the new-covenant Sabbath; the seventh day was but its shadow.

In the foregoing I have treated the subject of the shadowy Sabbath and its typical relation to our sweet, heavenly rest enjoyed on the bosom of divine love, the rich experience of the Christian in the gospel dispensation. But the rest which we now enter by faith is merely the foretaste of the eternal rest to be enjoyed in the hereafter. The language of Hebrews 4 clearly shows that the mind of the apostle was carried heavenward and included what Baxter was pleased to call *"the saints' eternal rest."*

God's family in heaven and on earth is one (Eph. 3:15). The kingdom of grace here and the kingdom of glory above express the endless reign of Christ, and is properly the great "kingdom of heaven." The Christian church of the present dispensation is properly termed the heavenly Jerusalem, and yet in Revelation 21 and 22, under the figure of the New Jerusalem, heaven with all its glory is opened to our view. In this life the redeemed are exalted to the plane of heaven and are said to be sitting in heavenly places in Christ Jesus, yet they live in bright anticipation of some day entering heaven itself, the eternal home of the redeemed. At death the departing saints return to the Lord "that they may rest from their labors; and their works do follow them" (Rev. 14:13). In that land of everlasting life "the wicked cease from troubling; and there the weary be at rest. There the prisoners rest together; they hear not the voice of the oppressor. The small and great are there; and the servant is free from his master" (Job 3:17-19). There is no question that the writer of Hebrews 4 included this future, eternal rest in his exhortation to the church to "labor therefore to enter into that rest, lest any man fall after the same example of unbelief." The law Sabbath, as well as Canaan, foreshadowed our rest in Christ, which begins here with salvation and continues in heaven forever.

The Old and New Sabbaths Contrasted

1.   The shadowy Sabbath was the observance of every seventh day. "The seventh day is the Sabbath" (Exod. 20:10). The new-covenant Sabbath is not the observance of this

particular day. "One man [the Jew] esteemeth one day above another: another [the Gentile Christian] esteemeth every day alike. Let every man be fully persuaded in his own mind....He that regardeth not the day, to the Lord he doth not regard it" (Rom. 14:5, 6). "Ye observe days....I am afraid of you" (Gal. 4:10, 11). "Let no man therefore judge you in respect...of the sabbath-days" (Col. 2:16)). These texts refer particularly to law days.

2.   The old was a rest of the body but one day in seven. The new is a rest of our souls every day. "For he that is entered into his rest, he also hath ceased from his own works, as God did from his" (Heb. 4:10). After God finished creation's work, he rested the seventh day. But his rest did not stop there. He rested the eighth, ninth, tenth, eleventh, twelfth day, and he has been resting from creation's work ever since. So we who have entered his rest cease from our works—self efforts—and enjoy a perpetual soul-rest.

3.   The old was a bodily rest, a temporal rest. The new is a spiritual rest that we enter by faith (Matt. 11:28, 29; Heb. 4:1-11), and is eternal.

4.   The old was enjoined in the law, and was binding upon Israel as a nation (Exod. 16:29; 31:13). The new is found in Christ under the new covenant and is to be enjoyed by all nations.

5.   Under the law but one day in seven was kept holy (Exod. 20:8, 10). Under the gospel we keep *every day* holy (Luke 1:74, 75).

6.   Total abstinence from manual labor constituted a holy day—Sabbath—to the Jews (Deut. 5:14). Abstinence from manual work does not make a day holy or unholy to us under the gospel (Rom. 14:5, 6; Gal. 4:10, 11; Col. 2:16). By totally abstaining, ceasing from our self-works, and living a righteous life, we keep every day holy (Heb. 4:10; Luke 1:74, 75). In the former the people totally abstained from manual work; while in the latter we cease from self-strivings, and enter the glorious rest of a perfect salvation.

7.   By performing the least amount of manual work on the seventh day, the Jews broke their Sabbath, and were stoned to death (Num. 15:32-36). By indulging in the least amount of sin, we now lose our sweet Sabbath rest, and spiritual death is the result (1 John 3:8; Jas. 1:15).

8.   The old was a "shadow" or type of the new (Col. 2:14-16; Heb. 4:1-11).

The Lord's Day

While John was on the Isle of Patmos he testified, "I was in the Spirit on the Lord's Day" (Rev. 1:10). This is the first place in the Bible that we have the expression "Lord's Day." John wrote this language sixty-six years after the Jewish Sabbath was abolished; hence he must have referred to some memorial day peculiar to the new dispensation. Never once was the seventh day ever termed the "Lord's Day"; "Sabbath" was the term always applied to that day. In not one single instance in the Bible or in history can a passage be found where the term "Lord's Day" is applied to the Jewish Sabbath. Sabbatarians themselves never call the seventh day the "Lord's Day" (except when they attempt to explain away "the Lord's Day" in Rev. 1:10); but in all their teachings, writings, and conversations, they say "Sabbath Day." The word "sabbath" is not used in Rev. 1:10. The Sabbath Day was abolished at the cross (Col. 2:14-16; Gal. 4:10; Rom. 14:5), more than sixty years before John wrote on Patmos; therefore, he could not have referred to that day. Another fact worthy of note here is that immediately after John's time whenever the term "Lord's Day" was used by the early church it was always applied to Sunday, and never once to the Sabbath.

In the New Testament we have "the blood of the Lord," "this cup of the Lord," "the disciples of the Lord," "the Lord's table," "the Lord's death," "the Lord's body," "the Lord's Supper," and "the Lord's Day." All these expressions refer to something that belongs to Christ exclusively under the gospel. Every intelligent person can at a glance comprehend this fact.

The Lord's Day is a memorial day, a day of commemoration. People keep days because of what occurred on them. For example: We in the United States celebrate the fourth day of each July to commemorate the signing of the Declaration of Independence. So has every nation its memorial days. Religion as well as nations has erected certain memorials to commemorate great events in her history. In the old dispensation the seventh day of the week was a holy sabbath for Israel and was also a memorial day to them, commemorating their deliverance from Egypt. Pentecost and the Passover were also memorial days. Would it not be strange, then, that the grandest of all institutions, the gospel, should have no memorials?

The two greatest events that ever occurred on earth we have in the gospel. They are the death and the resurrection of Jesus Christ. The salvation of all mankind centers in Christ's *death* and *resurrection.* All other events fade into mere insignificance when compared with these. Two monuments have been erected in the Christian age to commemorate these events. They are "the Lord's Supper" and "the Lord's Day." The first is in "remembrance" of his death; the last commemorates his resurrection. The Lord's Supper is to show his death "till he come"; the Lord's Day is a day of holy convocation, a day of rejoicing and spiritual devotion, because "he is risen." Tertullian, one of the early Christian writers, says, "We celebrate Sunday as a joyful day."

The Great Memorial Day of the Gospel

There is nothing in the events of Saturday—the seventh day—to inspire a Christian under the gospel. Christ was in the tomb. A guard of Roman soldiers were carefully watching the place. A sable gloom hung over the scene, and the pall of death cast its dark shadow. Yes, the world's Savior lay under the power of death. His body rested in the sepulcher and his soul was in Hades. It was a restless and disheartening day to the disconsolate disciples. When their Lord was buried their hopes died with him (Luke 24:17-21). It was a day of mourning and sadness. The disciples are weeping, Mary the mother is heart-broken, and if ever hell rejoiced and demons shouted it was on that Saturday. The remembrance of that day would always be a grievous one to the church. It would recall the agonies of death, the cross, the bitter cries, the expiring groan, and the mournful sepulcher. It would ever after create a feeling of sorrow. Yes, the events of that day—that Jewish Sabbath Day—have forever spoiled it to the Christian heart. Think of it, the wicked Jews were rejoicing and Satan triumphing! If ever the devil had hope, it was while Jesus was dead, during the Sabbath Day.

But as the first day of the week—Sunday—begins to dawn, a mighty angel like lightning descends, the earth quakes, the guards fall like dead men, the stone rolls away, the tomb opens, and Christ arises a conqueror over death, hell, and the grave (Matt. 28:1-4). Satan's last hope is gone; the wicked Jews are dismayed; the holy women are glad; the hope of the disciples is revived; angels rejoice; the salvation of a world is secured; the sufferings and humiliation of the Son of God are ended, and he walks forth the Almighty Savior, the Lord of all. This is *The Resurrection Day*. No wonder it became the memorial day of the church. It was impossible it should be otherwise.

It was the resurrection day on which everything turned. Jesus might have lived the pure life he did, might have wrought all the miracles he did, might have died on the cross as he did, might have been buried as he was, yet all this would not have saved a soul if he had not risen from the dead. "If Christ be not raised, your faith is vain; you are yet in your sins. Then they also which are fallen asleep in Christ are perished" (1 Cor. 15:17, 18). The resurrection completed the work which made Jesus both Savior and Lord. Jesus himself, when asked for the evidence of his authority, pointed to his resurrection on the third day as the proof of it (John 2:18-21; Matt. 12:28-40; 16-21). Paul says that Jesus was "declared to be the Son of God with power, according to the spirit of holiness, *by the resurrection from the dead*" (Rom. 1:4). It was this that proved his divinity. It was this that converted his own brethren in the flesh. Prior to the resurrection

"his brethren believed not on him." That there will be a final day
of judgment God "hath given assurance unto all men, in that he
hath raised him from the dead" (Acts 17:31).

"I will praise thee: for thou hast heard me, and art become
my salvation. The stone which the builders refused is become the
headstone of the corner. This is the Lord's doing; it is marvelous
in our eyes. This is the day which the Lord hath made: we will
rejoice and be glad in it" (Ps. 118:21-24).

Christ only is our hope and salvation. Him the Jews rejected
and put to death. To the third day he lay in the tomb, and the
sorrowful disciples said, "We trusted that it had been he which
should have redeemed Israel" (Luke 24:21). With his death, all
their hopes seem to have expired. All was lost. But on the third
day after the crucifixion they heard of his resurrection. Mary saw
the Lord and told the rest. Though their faith was weak, hope
began to revive. In the evening they were drawn together in
assembly. Behold, he appeared in their midst. So it is true the
Lord has risen! His resurrection confounds the Jews who
rejected and crucified him. The stone they had rejected suddenly
triumphs and becomes the head of the corner. He in whom they
had hoped and trusted for redemption has actually now "become
their salvation." "This is the Lord's doing; it is marvelous in our
eyes. *This is the day which the Lord hath made;* we will rejoice
and be glad in it." The great day of triumph, when Jesus rose
from the dead, is "the day which the Lord hath made"; hence
John rightly terms it the *"Lord's Day."* A day when all the
Christian world from the resurrection to this time have been led
to set apart for the assembling together in prayer and praise to
God. "In it we will rejoice and be glad," said the prophet. "We
celebrate Sunday as a joyful day," said Tertullian, one of the
primitive church fathers. And so say the redeemed of the Lord
generally.

As before observed, we keep days because of what occurred
on them. Two of the mightiest events in the history of
Christianity and the church occurred upon the first day of the
week—Christ's resurrection, and Pentecost. The great outpour-

ing of the Holy Spirit as recorded in Acts 2, the dedication of the new covenant sanctuary—church—its complete organization as a distinct body, the marvelous conversion of three thousand souls, all took place on this day. Jesus had said that "repentance and remission of sins should be preached in his name among all nations, *beginning at Jerusalem.*" This great and ever-widening stream of salvation work destined to become "a great mountain and fill the whole earth," and finally "cover the earth as the waters cover the sea," had its "beginning at Jerusalem." Pentecost was the fountain-head; and Pentecost was *on the first day of the week.* We humbly ask: How could it be otherwise that this day should become a memorial day to the Christian church? The *Resurrection, Pentecost,* and the *first day of the week* are always associated together in the Christian's mind.

It is *not the day* but *the events that occurred on the day* that we Christians celebrate. One day is not a whit better than another. One day is no more holy than another. This we have abundantly proved. It is not Sunday, because it is Sunday, that we keep—it is the *resurrection day,* the *Pentecostal day,* and this occurred upon "the first day of the week"—Sunday. Had these events occurred upon Monday, Tuesday, Wednesday, or any other day, then that day would become memorial in the Christian's mind. So our salvation does not depend upon monumental ordinances. But just as each first day of the week comes around to us in all parts of the world, we follow the apostolic examples of celebrating the resurrection of our Lord, and set apart the day for worship and spiritual devotion. We dispense with our temporal responsibilities and devote the day to the Lord, to his worship. Hence to us as well as to the early Christians it is *the "Lord's day."*

First Day Observance

Adventists are continually crying, "Sunday is the pope's day." They tell the people that it was the pope who started the observance of the first day of the week; that the Sabbath was observed by all Christians until the pope's time; and that it was he who changed the keeping of days from the seventh to the first. Almost all Sabbatarians are ignorantly led into this belief, and they are constantly heard to affirm that those who observe the Lord's Day are keeping the pope's day—"a heathen day, the venerable day of the sun," etc. Such talk betrays great ignorance to the enlightened and informed. We have but to attend to the evidences in the case to prove that this is all assumption. The united testimony of the early Christian church, centuries before there was a pope elected, proves that the first day of the week was regularly observed as a memorial and sacred day. I do not quote those early church writers to prove a doctrine (I go to the Bible for that); but I simply quote them to prove a historical fact; namely, that the early Christians did keep Sunday as a sacred day.

A. D. 30—THE RESURRECTION DAY

"And they rose up the same hour, and returned to Jerusalem, and found the eleven gathered together, and them that were with them, saying, The Lord is risen indeed" (Luke 24:33, 34). This was the first day of the week, the day on which Christ arose (see John 20:19). "And as they thus spake, Jesus himself stood in the midst of them, and saith unto them, Peace be unto you" (Luke 24:36).

ONE WEEK LATER, OR THE NEXT SUNDAY

"And after eight days again his disciples were within, and Thomas with them; then came Jesus, the doors being shut, and stood in the midst, and said, Peace be unto you" (John 20:26).

PENTECOST—ACTS 2

The feast of Pentecost was on the "morrow after the seventh sabbath" (Lev. 23:15, 16). That would be the first day of the week. "And when the Day of Pentecost was fully come, they were all with one accord in one place" (Acts 2:1). "The number of names together were about an hundred and twenty" (Acts 1:15).

A. D. 59—ACTS 20:6, 7

"And upon the first day of the week, when the disciples came together to break bread, Paul preached unto them."

1 COR. 16:1, 2

"Now concerning the collection for the saints, as I have given order to the churches of Galatia, even so do ye. Upon the first day of the week let every one of you lay by him in store, as God hath prospered him, that there be no gatherings when I come."

A. D. 96—REV. 1:10

"I was in the Spirit on the Lord's Day."

A. D. 107—PLINY'S LETTER

Pliny wrote to Trajan concerning the Christians: "They were wont to meet together, on *a stated day* before it was light, and sang among themselves alternately a hymn to Christ as God."— *Home's Introduction* (vol. 1, chap. 3, sec. 2, p. 84). Early in the morning the Christians assemblèd—"before it was light." These meetings were on a "certain stated day." On what day were the early morning meetings held? Eusebius the historian answers: "By this is prophetically signified the service which is performed very early and every morning *of the resurrection day throughout* the whole world."—*Sabbath Manual* (p. 125). The day on which Christ rose was the "stated day" on which the Christians met for worship. Pliny was governor of Bithynia, Asia Minor, A. D. 106-108. This was the very place where the apostles labored, and the time only eleven years after John died.

(Much of the following in this chapter is compiled from various works, principally from *Seventh-day Adventism Renounced,* by Canright.)

A. D. 120—BARNABAS

This epistle was highly prized in the earliest churches, and is found in the oldest manuscript of the Scriptures; namely, the Sinaitic.

Elder Andrews, a Seventh-day Adventist, admits that the Epistle of Barnabas "was in existence as early as the middle of the second century, and, like the 'Apostolic Constitutions,' is of value to us in that it gives some clue to the opinions which prevailed in the region where the writer lived." — *Testimony of the Fathers* (p. 21).

"The epistle is believed to have been written early in the second *century.* "—*Smith's Dictionary of the Bible.*

"This work is unanimously ascribed to Barnabas, the companion of St. Paul, by early Christian writers....But the great majority of critics assign it to the reign of Hadrian sometime between 119 and 126 A. D." — *Encyclopedia Brittanica.*

"The epistle was probably written in Alexandria at the beginning of the second century and by a Gentile Christian." — *Schaff-Herzog Encyclopedia.*

It "is supposed by Hefele to have been written between 107-120 A. D." —*Johnson's New Universal Cyclopedia.*

This is a summary of the best modern criticism as to the date, character, and authority of the Epistle of Barnabas. Read and reverenced in the church as early as A. D. 120, or within twenty-four years of the death of John, it shows what Christians believed and practiced immediately after the apostles. In this epistle we read, "Incense is a vain abomination unto me, and your new moons and sabbaths I cannot endure. He has, therefore, abolished these things" (chap. 2).

Coming to the first day of the week, Barnabas says: "Wherefore, also, we keep the eighth day with joyfulness, the day, also, on which Jesus rose again from the dead" (chap. 15). Will the Adventists say that there was a pope in A. D. 120? Hardly. Yet the Christians kept the resurrection day with joyfulness.

A. D. 125—THE TEACHING OF THE APOSTLES

"But every Lord's Day do ye gather yourselves together, and break bread, and give thanksgiving" (chap. 14). Notice how this harmonizes with Acts 20:6, 7: "And upon the first day of the week, when the disciples came together to break bread."

A. D. 140—JUSTIN MARTYR

Justin Martyr wrote about forty-four years after John died. He held his "Dialog with Trypho" at Ephesus, Asia Minor, in the church where St. John lived and died.

His first defense of the Christian religion is addressed to the emperor Antoninus Verus. In the introduction to his writings in the "Ante-Nicene Library" the writer says, "The first class embraces those which are *unquestionably genuine; viz.*, the two *Apologies,* and the *Dialog with Trypho."*

In *Eusebius' Ecclesiastical History,* which is the first historical work written after the close of the inspired record is found a statement of the books of Justin that had come down to Eusebius' time. Says the historian (Book 4, chap. 18), "Another work comprising a defense of our faith, which he addressed to the emperor of the same name, Antoninus Verus." Here the genuineness of this work of Justin's is established beyond the shadow of a doubt. "Before his conversion to God he studied in the schools of philosophy." "The writings of Justin Martyr are among the most important that have come down to us from the second century.' *—Ante-Nicene Library.*

He speaks to us from the first half of the second century. We quote from his first defense or apology, which we have seen is acknowledged by *Eusebius' Ancient History.* The head of this article is—"Chapter 67. *The weekly worship of the Christians.* "And on the day called Sunday, all who live in cities or in the country gather together to one place, and the memoirs of the apostles or the writings of the prophets are read as long as time permits.

"And they who are well-to-do, and willing, give what each thinks fit: and what is collected is deposited with the president, who succors the orphans and widows, and those, who through sickness or any other cause, are in want, and those who are in bonds, and the strangers sojourning among us, and in a word takes care of all who are in need. *But Sunday is the day on which we all hold our common assembly,* because it is the first day on which God, having wrought a change in the darkness and matter, made the world; and Jesus Christ our Savior on the same day rose from the dead. For he was crucified on the day before that of Saturn (Saturday), and on the day after that of Saturn, which is the day of the sun, having appeared to his apostles and disciples, he taught them these things, which we have submitted to you also for your consideration." You perceive that Justin describes the weekly worship of the early church just as Paul directed, on Sunday, or the first day of the week, in 1 Corinthians 16.

Our next quotation is from his *Dialog with Trypho.* Of the genuineness of this work we have the most positive historical evidence. Eusebius, (Book 4, chap. 18), says, "He [Justin] also wrote a dialog against the Jews which he held at Ephesus with Trypho, the most distinguished among the Hebrews of the day." In such a disputation would very naturally be brought out the very points at issue between Jews and Christians then, and between Christians and all who now occupy common ground with the Jews. In other words, if the early Christians kept the old law, or any part of it, that would be urged by them as a means of procuring respect for, and confidence in, the Christian system from Jewish quarters. On the other hand, if the primitive Christians utterly discarded the whole Sinaitic law and the seventh-day Sabbath, then we might expect Jewish prejudices arising therefrom, and the Christians put to the necessity of giving their reasons for abandoning that ancient law and Sabbath. Hence this discussion between Justin, an eminent Christian and philosopher, and Trypho, a learned Jew, is of important service to us, on all points of difference between Christians and Jews. And we shall find that it contains in abundance the very matter we have anticipated. We quote from—

"Chapter 10. *Trypho blames the Christians for this alone—the nonobservance of the law.*

"And when they ceased, I again addressed them thus: 'Is there any other matter, my friend, in which we are blamed than this, that we live not after the law, and we are not circumcised in the flesh as your forefathers were, and *do not observe Sabbaths as ye do?'"* To this Trypho replied as follows: "I am aware that your precepts in the so-called gospel are so wonderful and so great that I suspect no one can keep them; for I have carefully read them. But this is what we are most at a loss about: that you, professing to be pious, and supposing yourselves better than others, are not in any particular separated from them, and do not alter your mode of living from the nations, in that you observe no festivals or sabbaths, and do not have the rite of circumcision; and further, resting your hopes on a man that was crucified, you yet expect to obtain some good thing from God while you do not obey his commandments."

Trypho had read the precepts of the gospel. He was not quite so law-blinded as modern law-teachers. He could see precepts in the gospel. He saw that Christ had given a new law, and it impressed his mind as "wonderful and great"; that is, very high and pure—"so great that I suspect no man can keep it." He saw the truth but knew not that "grace and truth" came together. Observe, also, that Trypho viewed the law Sabbath in the light in which the Bible places it; namely, as the badge of separation from all other nations. And since the Christians rejected the Sabbath, he accused them of not being separate from other nations. He accused Justin just as the Adventists now accuse Christians: i. e., of disobeying God's commandments.

The next reply is headed as follows:

"Chapter 11. *The law abrogated; the new testament promised and given by God.*

"'There will be no other God, O Trypho, nor was there from eternity any other existing,'...'but he who made and disposed all this universe....But we do not trust through Moses, or through the law, for then we would do the same as yourselves. But now—(for I have read that there shall be a final law, and a covenant, the chiefest of all, which it is now incumbent on all men to observe, as many as are seeking after the inheritance of God. For the law promulgated on Horeb is old, and belongs to *yourselves alone;* but *this* is for all universally. Now, law placed against law *has abrogated that which is before it,* and a covenant which comes after in like manner has *put an end to the previous one* [Is not this just what the Word says—"Christ is the end of the law for righteousness to all them that believe"?]; and an eternal and final law—namely, Christ—has been given to us, and the covenant is trustworthy, after which there shall be no law, no commandment, no ordinance. Have you not read this which Isaiah says? "Hearken unto me, hearken unto me, my people; and ye kings, give ear unto me: for a law shall go forth from me, and my judgment shall be for a light to the nations. My righteousness approaches swiftly, and my salvation shall go forth, and nations shall trust in mine arm." And by Jeremiah concerning this same new covenant, he thus speaks: "Behold, the days come, saith the Lord, that I will make a new covenant with the house of Israel, and with the house of Judah; not according to the covenant which I made with their fathers in the day that I took them by the hand to bring them out of the land of Egypt.") If, therefore, God proclaimed a new covenant which was to be instituted, and this for the light of the nations, we see and are persuaded that men approach God, leaving their idols and other unrighteousness, through the name of him who was crucified, Jesus Christ, and abide by their confession even unto death, and maintain piety. Moreover, by the works and by the attendant miracles, it is possible for all to understand that he is the new law, and the new covenant, and the expectation of those who out of every people wait for the good things of God. For the true spiritual Israel and descendants of Judah, Jacob, Isaac, and Abraham (who in uncircumcision was approved of and blessed by God on account of his faith, and called the father of many nations) are we who have been led to God through the crucified Christ, as shall be demonstrated while we proceed.'

"Chapter 12. *The Jews violate the eternal law, and interpret ill that of Moses.*

"I also adduced another passage in which Isaiah exclaims: 'Hear my words, and your soul shall live; and I will make an everlasting covenant with you, even the sure mercies of David....' " This same law you have despised, and this holy covenant you have slighted; and now you neither receive it, nor repent of your evil deeds. 'For your ears are closed, your eyes are blinded, and the heart is hardened,' Jeremiah has cried; yet not even then do you listen. The Lawgiver is present, yet you do not see him; to the poor the gospel is preached, the blind see, yet you do not understand. You have now need of a second circumcision, though you glory greatly in the flesh. The new law requires you to keep *perpetual sabbath, and you, because you are idle for one* day, suppose you are pious, not discerning why this has been commanded you; and if you eat unleavened bread, you say the will of God has been fulfilled. The Lord our God does not take pleasure in such observances: if there is any perjured person or a thief among you, let him cease to be so; if any adulterer, let him repent; *then he has kept the sweet and true sabbath of God.* If anyone has impure hands, let him wash and be pure."

We next quote from—

"Chapter 18. *Christians would observe the law, if they did not know why it was instituted.*

"'For we too would observe the fleshly circumcision and the sabbaths, and in short all the feasts, if we did not know for what reason they were enjoined on you,—namely on account of your transgressions and the hardness of your hearts. For if we patiently endure all things contrived against us by wicked men and demons, so that even amid cruelties unutterable, death and torments, we pray for mercy to those who inflict such things upon us, and do not wish to give the least retort to anyone, even as the new Lawgiver commanded us: how is it Trypho, that we should not observe those rites which do not harm us,—I speak of fleshly circumcision, and sabbaths, and feasts?'

"Therefore to you alone this circumcision was necessary, in order that the people may be no people, and the nation no nation; as also Hosea, one of the twelve prophets, declares. Moreover, all those righteous men already mentioned, *though they kept no Sabbaths,* were pleasing to God."

"And you were commanded to keep sabbaths that you might

retain the memorial of God."

The next chapter from which we quote is headed as follows: "Chapter 21. *Sabbaths were instituted on account of the people's sins, and not for a work of righteousness.*

"'Moreover, that God enjoined you to keep the Sabbath, and imposed on you other precepts for a sign, as I have already said, on account of your unrighteousness and that of your fathers' …'Wherefore I gave them also statutes which were not good, and judgments whereby they shall not live.'

The next quotation is from—

"Chapter 23. *The opinion of the Jews regarding the law does an injury to God.*

"'But if we do not admit this, we shall be liable to fall into foolish opinions, as if it were not the same God who existed in the times of Enoch and all the rest, *who neither were circumcised after the flesh, nor observed Sabbaths,* nor any other rites, seeing that *Moses enjoined such observances;* or that God had not wished each race of mankind continually to perform the same righteous actions: to admit which seems to be ridiculous and absurd. Therefore we must confess that he, who is ever the same, has commanded these and such like institutions on account of sinful men.'"

Dear reader, consider these things. The law-teachers of our day tell us that the immutability of God requires that the law given on Sinai must be the unchangeable standard of righteousness. But Justin reminds us that God counted the patriarchs righteous before the law was given on Sinai; and, therefore, if he afterward measured righteousness by the Sinaitic law, this would prove God changeable. So to make the Sinaitic code a standard of righteousness, slanders the character of God. But just as the New Testament teaches,—that righteousness is not by the law (Gal. 3:21); that Abraham, who lived before the law, is set before us as the example for our faith and righteousness; that he is indeed the father of the faithful; that all who believe in Christ are the seed of Abraham (Rom. 4:3-22; Gal. 3:29); and that all who seek to be righteous by the law fail to attain unto righteousness

(Rom. 9:31; 10:3)—we say, just as the New Testament rules out the law written on stone as a means to or standard of righteousness, so does Justin. As the apostles teach us that the law was not given for righteous men, but for the ungodly, and because of transgressions; so Justin proves the unchangeableness of God by showing that his law of righteousness was substantially the same in holy men before Moses and in the gospel dispensation since the Mosaic system has passed away, and that the law was simply a temporary code for the restraint of the wicked. Under the head, *"The law was given by Moses on account of the hardness of their hearts,"* Justin says, "Until Moses, under whom your nation appeared unrighteous and ungrateful to God, making a calf in the wilderness: wherefore God accommodated himself to that nation"; that is, in giving them the law that he did. Thus, we see the immutability of God vindicated both by the Scriptures and by the early writers of the church of God, by leaving the law code out of the question, and basing righteousness before and after it upon the same general principles. Even though Abraham was circumcised, the apostle is very particular to inform us that his righteousness, which is the same as ours, was that ascribed to him before he was circumcised (Rom. 4:9-11).

But let us continue to hear Justin. "Wherefore, Trypho, I will proclaim to you, and to those who wish to become proselyte, the divine message which I heard from that man. Do you see that the elements are not idle and keep no sabbaths? Remain as you were born. For If there was no need of circumcision before Abraham, *or the observance of* sabbaths, or feasts and sacrifices *before Moses,* no more need is there of them now, after that, according to the will of God, Jesus Christ the Son of God, has been born without sin, of a virgin springing from the stock of Abraham."

Observe that Justin always associates the Sabbath of the Jews with feasts, sacrifices, etc., the shadows or ceremonies of the law. Just so does Paul in Col. 2:14, 16, 17, where the apostle classifies it with meats and drinks, and tells us that persons converted from the Jews to Christ are as much at liberty to disregard the Sabbath of the abrogated code as its discrimination in meats. It is almost always mentioned in the Old Testament with that class of precepts, such as reverencing the sanctuary (Lev. 19:30), the celebration of national feasts, "her feast-days, her new moons, and her sabbaths, and all her solemn feasts" (Hosea 2:11). In Ezek. 45:17 it is associated with "burnt offerings, and meat-offerings, and drink offerings, in the feasts, and in the new moons, and in the sabbaths."

Observe again, Justin shows that the Sabbath of the law was out of harmony with the laws of nature, hence one of the "statutes he had given them that was not good, and judgments whereby they should not live" (Ezek. 20:25). The elements keep no Sabbath. To remain inactive a whole day was contrary to nature; and yet to labor was death.

Observe, too, that Justin speaks of the sabbath of the gospel as a "sweet" and *"perpetual sabbath."* By this he shows that it is not the observance of any day, but a spiritual rest of the soul. This spiritual rest he further says is the *"true sabbath of God."* To this we say amen. The Lord's Day is not a sabbath, but a memorial day. It is, by the leading of the Spirit, a day of great activity in the vineyard of the Lord.

The next chapter from Justin is—

"Chapter 24. *The Christians' circumcision far more excellent.*

"'Now, sirs,' I said, 'it is possible for us to show how *the eighth day possessed a certain mysterious import which the seventh day did not possess,* and which was promulgated by God through these rites. But lest I appear now to diverge to other subjects understand what I say: the blood of that circumcision is obsolete, and we trust in the blood of salvation; *there is now another covenant, and another law has gone forth from Zion.'* "

Our next quotation is from—

"Chapter 43. *He concludes that the law had an end in Christ.*

"'As, then, circumcision began with Abraham, and *the*

Sabbath and sacrifices and offerings and feasts *with Moses,* and it has been proved they were enjoined on account of the hardness of your people's hearts, so it was necessary in accordance with the Father's will, that they should have an end in Him who was born of a virgin.'

A question (chap. 47), "And Trypho again inquired, 'But if someone, knowing that this is so, after he recognizes that this man is Christ, and has believed in and obeys him, wishes, however, to observe these [institutions of the law], will he be saved?'

"I said, 'In my opinion, Trypho, such an one will be saved, if he does not strive in every way to persuade other men...to observe the same things as himself.'

Here again we see the very sentiment of the Apostle. "Let not him that eateth not judge him that eateth," etc. "He that is weak eateth herbs." Just so, "One man esteemeth one day above another: another esteemeth every day alike. Let everyone be fully persuaded in his own mind. He that regardeth the day, regardeth it unto the Lord; and he that regardeth not the day, to the Lord he doth not regard it. He that eateth, eateth to the Lord, for he giveth God thanks; and he that eateth not, to the Lord he eateth not, and giveth God thanks" (Rom. 14:5, 6).

How very different this sounds from the old Sabbath law! It imperatively commands abstinence from all labor on the seventh day, under penalty of death; while the apostle gives liberty to "esteem every day alike," and allows everyone to be "fully persuaded in his own mind," whether to regard one day more specially unto the Lord than another. Both he that does so and he that does not are recognized as pleasing the Lord and being accepted of him. Can anyone imagine that the old "ministration of death" and "yoke of bondage," and this new-testament "law of liberty," can both blend into one system, and be in force at the same time? The old would be a cold, grating discord in the government of this dispensation.

But let us return and read Justin's answer to this question a little further. He says: "But if some, through weakmindedness,

wish to observe such institutions as were given by Moses, for
which they expect some virtue, but which we believe were
appointed by reason of the hardness of the people's hearts, along
with their hope in this Christ, and [wish to perform] the eternal
and natural acts of righteousness and piety, yet choose to live
with the Christians and the faithful, as I said before, not inducing
them either to be circumcised like themselves, or to keep the
Sabbath, or to observe any other such ceremonies, then I hold
that we ought to join ourselves to such, and associate with them
in all things as kinsmen and brethren."

Here Justin ascribes the disposition of persons to hold on to
the old law and to observe the Sabbath after professing faith in
Christ, to ignorance. He also teaches that "eternal and natural"
law of righteousness of which the apostle speaks in Romans,
originally written in man's conscience, and perfectly covered by
the law of Christ; whereas the law containing the Sabbath is no
part of that natural internal law of our moral being, but a
temporary restraint against sin, occasioned by hardness of heart.

Again, we observe that Justin expressed the very sentiments
of the inspired Apostle when he said that such might be saved,
and should be received by the church, as through ignorance, still
held to the law, and kept that Sabbath, provided they also
evinced the humble spirit of Christ and did not seek to propagate
their notions. "If he does not strive in every way to persuade
other men" under the yoke of the law. The Adventists do the
very thing he says they must not do, and indeed, the very thing
that brings them under the apostolic curse (Gal. 1:8, 9).

Here we leave Justin, having heard enough in his discussion
with Trypho to corroborate strongly all that is said in the New
Testament about the end of the old law and its Sabbath, and the
fact that the first day of the week is the Lord's Day.

A. D. 170—DIONYSIUS, BISHOP OF CORINTH IN GREECE

This elder was not from Rome, but from Greece. He says, "We
passed this holy Lord's Day, in which we read your letter,"
etc.—Eusebius' Ecclesiastical History, (Book IV, chap. 23).

A. D. 194—CLEMENT OF ALEXANDRIA, EGYPT

"He, in fulfillment of the precept, keeps the Lord's Day when he abandons an evil disposition, and assumes that of the Gnostic, glorifying the Lord's resurrection in himself" (Book VII, chap. 12).

It will be seen that these early writers all refer to the resurrection day as the Lord's Day.

A. D. 200—TERTULLIAN OF AFRICA

"Let him who contends that the Sabbath is still to be observed...teach us that for the past time righteous men kept the Sabbath." "God originated Adam uncircumcised and in observant of the Sabbath."—Answer *to the Jews* (chap. 2). "The observance of the Sabbath is demonstrated to have been temporary" (chap. 4).

"We solemnize *the day after Saturday* in contradistinction to those who call this day their *Sabbath.*"—*Tertullian's Apology* (chap. 16).

At this early date Saturday was utterly disregarded, while Sunday was observed.

A. D. 225—ORIGEN

Origen's home was in Egypt, and he traveled all over the East, and died in Tyre. Hear him: "If it be objected to us on this subject that we ourselves are accustomed to observe certain days, as, for example, the Lord's Day."— *Origen against Celsus* (Book VIII, chap. 22).

A. D. 250—THE APOSTOLICAL CONSTITUTIONS

"And on the day of our Lord's resurrection, which is the Lord's Day, meet more diligently, sending praise to God." "Otherwise what apology will he make to God who does not assemble on that day to hear the saving word concerning the resurrection" (sec. 7, par. 59).

"On the day of the resurrection of the Lord, that is, the Lord's Day, assemble yourselves together, without fail, giving thanks to God." "On which account we solemnly assemble to celebrate the feast of the resurrection of the Lord's Day" (Book VII, sec. 2, par. 30).

This testimony at this early date is conclusive. It utterly refutes the Adventist absurdity that Sunday observance started with the pope.

A. D. 270—ANATOLIUS, BISHOP OF LAODICEA, ASIA

He was a Greek. Hear him: "The solemn festival of the resurrection of the Lord can be celebrated only on the Lord's Day" (Tenth Canon).

"Our regard for the Lord's resurrection, which took place on the Lord's Day, will lead us to celebrate it on the same principle" (Sixteenth Canon).

Again the resurrection day is called "the Lord's Day."

A. D. 300—VICTORINUS, BISHOP OF PETAU

"On the Lord's Day we go forth to our bread with giving of thanks. And let the parasceve become a rigorous fast lest we should appear to observe any Sabbath with the Jews, which Christ himself, the Lord of Sabbath, says by his prophets that his soul hateth, which Sabbath he in his body abolished."—Creation *of the World* (sec. *4).*

A. D. 306—PETER, BISHOP OF ALEXANDRIA

"But the Lord's Day we celebrate as a day of joy, because on it he rose again" (Canon 15).

A. D. 324—EUSEBIUS

Eusebius bears the title of "Father of Church History." He was born in Palestine, the very home of Christ and the apostles, and the cradle of the early church. He was bishop of Caesarea, where Paul abode two years. He studied at Antioch, where Paul labored for years. He traveled to Egypt and over Asia Minor. He was one of the most noted men of his age. Adventists say that the Sabbath was changed to Sunday at the Council of Laodicea. But Eusebius, who wrote fifty years before this council was held, says, speaking of the patriarchs, "They did not, therefore, regard circumcision, *nor observe the Sabbath, neither do we*...because such things as these do not belong to *Christians."—Ecclesiastical History* (Book 1, chap. 4). This is decisive. A. D. 324 Christians did not keep the Sabbath.

"And all things whatsoever that it was the duty to do on the Sabbath, these we have transferred to the Lord's Day as more honorable than the Jewish Sabbath." He further says that "all nations redeemed by him throughout the world, after an interval of six days, assemble on this *day."—Sabbath Manual* (pages 126, 127).

This strong array of historical evidence has been cited in order to prove beyond question that the early Christian church from the very day Christ rose from the dead assembled together and held that day as a sacred memorial day. Mark the fact that all the foregoing historical testimony was written before there was a pope in power. These witnesses were not simply from Rome, but from all parts of the world—from Africa, Asia, and Europe. Their united testimony proves beyond doubt that the early Christians in all the world did keep Sunday, the Lord's Day, as a sacred day, and utterly disregarded the observance of the Jewish Sabbath. That Sunday observance began with the pope of Rome is a falsehood.

Following is additional testimony from high authorities. "The universal and uncontradicted Sunday observance in the second century can only be explained by the fact that it had its roots in apostolic practice."—Historij *of the Christian Church,* by Dr. Schaff (vol. 1, p. 478).

"For a time the Jewish converts observed both the seventh day, to which the name Sabbath continued to be given exclusively, and the first day, which came to be called the Lord's Day....Within a century after the death of the last apostles we find the observance of the first day of the week, under the name of the Lord's Day, established as a universal custom of the church....It was regarded, not as a continuation of the Jewish Sabbath [which was denounced together with circumcision and other Jewish and anti-Christian practices], but rather as a substitute for it, naturally its observance was based on the resurrection of Christ rather than on the creation restday. or the Sabbath of the *Decalog.*"—*Johnson's New Universal Cyclopedia* (Art. Sabbath).

"In the second century its [Sunday] observance was universal....The Jewish Christian ceased to observe the Sabbath after the destruction of *Jerusalem.*"—*Schaff-Herzog Encyclopedia* (Art. "Sunday").

"The results of our examination of the principal writers of the two centuries after the death of John, are as follows: The Lord's Day existed during these two centuries as a part and parcel of apostolical and so of Scriptural Christianity. It was never defended; for it was never impugned, or at least only impugned as were other things received from the apostles. *It was never confounded with the Sabbath, but carefully distinguished from it...*It was not an institution of severe Sabbatical character, but a day of joy and cheerfulness, rather encouraging than forbidding relaxation. Religiously regarded, it was a day of solemn meeting for the holy eucharist, for united prayer, for instruction, for almsgiving: and though being an institution under the law of liberty, work does not appear to have been formally interdicted, or rest formally enjoined. Tertullian seems to indicate that the character of the day was opposed to worldly business. Finally, whatever analogy may be supposed to exist between the Lord's Day and the Sabbath, in no passage that has come down to us is the fourth commandment appealed to as the ground of the obligation to observe the Lord's *Day.*"—*Smith's Dictionary of the Bible* (Art. "Lord's Day").

These eminent authorities, who have carefully investigated this point, unite in testifying that the early Christian church universally held the resurrection day—termed the "Lord's Day"—as a sacred day, on which they held their meetings. All this testimony proves that the Adventist talk about Sunday being the pope's day is only a scarecrow, and is as baseless as the shadow of a dream. The testimony of history that the Christian church universally held Sunday as a sacred day before the pope's time is so overwhelming that even Adventist writers are compelled to admit it. Hear their admissions:

Concerning the writings of Barnabas, from which I have quoted in the preceding pages, Andrews (Seventh-day Adventist) admits that it "was in existence as early as the middle of the second century, and, like the 'Apostolic Constitutions,' is of value to us in that it gives some clue to the opinions which prevailed in the region where the writer lived."—*Testimony of the Fathers* (page 21). Of the writings of Barnabas he admits that "he presently asserts the abolition of the Sabbath of the Lord."—*Testimonies* (page 22).

"The reasons offered by the early Fathers for neglecting the observance of the Sabbath show conclusively that they had no special light on the subject by reason of living in the first centuries."—History *of the Sabbath,* by Andrews (page 308). Andrews is acknowledged to be the ablest historian of the Seventh-day Adventists. Look at his admission: "The early Fathers" "in the first centuries" neglected "the observance of the Sabbath." This was hundreds of years before the pope was elected.

Why Christians Keep The Lord's Day

With the exception of a few small sects, Christians universally regard Sunday as a sacred day. This has been true down through the centuries from the days of the apostles. The greatest reformers, such as Luther, Melancthon, Zwingle, and Wesley, and great and good men like John Bunyan and John Milton, all wrote in favor of the observance of the Lord's Day. Surely there must be some good reasons for such a universal practice. Yes, we answer, and reasons which have been entirely satisfactory to the deepest and ablest Christians of the church down through the many centuries of the Christian era. A few of these reasons I shall now submit to the reader.

First. Since the Jewish Sabbath was abolished at the death of Christ, and we are now under a new dispensation, the greatest of all institutions—the gospel—the Lord has not left us without a memorial day, a day to commemorate the greatest of all events—the resurrection of Christ.

Let it be remembered that the observance of days as mere rest-days does not belong to the gospel system. The Sabbath of the gospel is our spiritual rest in Christ. The idea of Sabbath as enjoined in the law is not connected with the Lord's Day. The Gentile Christians never so regard it. All the early church writers exclude this idea of the Lord's Day. They simply held it sacred as a memorial day to commemorate Christ's resurrection. The church Fathers plainly state that they enjoyed a sweet perpetual Sabbath—meaning rest in Christ. I quote from *Smith's Dictionary of the Bible* (Art. "Lord's Day"): "It was not an institution of severe sabbatical character, but a day of joy and cheerfulness....Religiously regarded, it was a day of solemn meeting for the holy eucharist [communion], for united prayer, for instruction, for alms-giving; and though being an institution under the law of liberty, work does not appear to have been formally interdicted, or rest formally enjoined." This expresses exactly the manner in which the early church regarded the resurrection day. It was regarded as a day of rejoicing, convocation, religious devotion, in honor of the resurrection. At the present time most people through tradition regard the Lord's Day as a holy Sabbath Day. However, since the laws of our land enjoin abstinence in general from manual labor, we as a God-fearing people and law-abiding citizens observe the laws of our land in this respect. But religiously, we keep the Lord's Day only as the early church did—as a memorial day of rejoicing, and of religious assembly, in honor of the resurrection of Christ.

Second. In the inspired history of the church, which covers a period of about sixty-five years, not one exclusive meeting of the church of God on the seventh day is recorded. Every exclusive meeting held by the infant church in its virgin purity was upon the first day of the week, the Lord's day. "After the Lord Jesus had revealed himself to the two disciples with whom he had walked out to Emmaus the day of his resurrection, we are told,

'They rose up the same hour and returned to Jerusalem, and found the eleven gathered, and them that were with them' (Luke 24:33). Perhaps the entire hundred and twenty made up that assembly. Here, then, we have an example of the church assembled together in their own meeting. They may only have been drawn together by the Spirit of God. Nevertheless the fact is on record that the very day that Jesus rose from the dead they assembled together. And while the two disciples were rehearsing how the blessed Savior had made himself known to them, lo! 'Jesus himself stood in the midst of them and said unto them, Peace be unto you' (vs. 36). So the Lord met with them and blessed this first meeting.

"Should the Saturday-keeper say that this first meeting was after night, and therefore not on the first day, but the second, we shall let the Word of God answer 'Then the same day at evening, being the first day of the week, when the doors were shut where the disciples were assembled for fear of the Jews, came Jesus and stood in the midst, and saith unto them, Peace be unto you.' (John 20:19). It was the same day that Jesus rose, and how particular the Spirit of inspiration is to tell that it was on *'the first day of the week'!* It must, therefore, be conceded that they convened before the close of the Jewish day, or else the text proves that right there in the change of dispensation the Lord no longer reckoned the day to sunset, but included it in the first part of the night, as we do now. One thing is sure, this meeting of the infant church was on the resurrection day of our Lord.

"Neither is there a word said about their assembling on the next Saturday. But we are told, 'And after eight days again his disciples were within, and Thomas with them then came Jesus, the doors being shut, and stood in the midst, and said, Peace be unto you' (John 20:26). This evidently records a second meeting one week from the former. The Jews were familiar with the two great annual sabbaths connected with the feast of unleavened bread, called the 'first day' and 'the eighth day.'...What, therefore, would be more natural than the use of such language?

"'The same day, being the *first day,* the disciples were

assembled.' 'And after eight days again.' These expressions agree so perfectly with the language of Lev. 23:35, 36 that it would seem that they were selected purposely to connect in our minds type and antitype. 'On the first day shall be an holy convocation,' and 'on the eighth day shall be an holy convocation.' As certain as this eighth day was one week from the first day, so also the eighth day of John 20:26 was one week from the 'first day' of verse 19....'After eight days,' meaning after the arrival of the eighth day, very naturally fell into use to designate one week. The same expression is in common use to this day in the German language. Their regular way of saying in one week from today is *'Heute ueber acht Tage'*—today over eight days. So the disciples assembled together upon the eve of the resurrection day and in one week from that time again. Here starts in the weekly worship of the Christians so freely spoken of in early history."—*The Sabbath.*

"After eight days" compared with the expression "after three days" shows clearly that this meeting was held one week from the former. The number of days after Christ's death till the day on which he was to rise is expressed as follows: "in three days" (Matt. 26:61; 27:40); "the third day" (Matt. 16:21; 20:19); and "after three days" (Mark 8:31). Thus, in their mode of expression "three days," "the third day," "after three days," all meant the keep the first day of the week, the day upon which Jesus rose, and our life also sprang up.' Such was the uniform testimony of the early Fathers, and what little is said in the Word about these secondary elements of Christianity all agrees in exactly the same thing. 'Upon the first day of the week, when the disciples came together.' 'And on the first day of the week, when we had gathered together to break *bread.'*—*Rotherham.* The language clearly indicates that their meetings were regularly held on that day. It does not simply state that they held a meeting on that day, but fairly intimates that they were in the habit of doing so. *'When the disciples came together.'* This speaks as though it were a matter of course that they would assemble on that day. No such example can be found in the New Testament of the holy church meeting on Saturday. Nay, they passed it by and met on the Lord's Day.

"This communion meeting occurred in A. D. 60. The year before, the same apostle wrote his first Epistle to the Corinthians, in which he gave directions respecting their duty on the day as follows: 'Now concerning the collection for the saints, as I have given order to the churches of Galatia, even so do ye. Upon the first day of the week let every one of you lay by him in store, as God hath prospered him, that there be no gatherings when I come. And when I come, whomsoever ye shall approve by your letters, them will I send to bring your liberality unto Jerusalem' (1 Cor. 16:1-3). The subject is 'concerning collections for the saints.' The word 'collections,' financially speaking, means the gathering of means together into a treasury, ready to be disbursed for the designed object. This collection was to be taken up on the first day of the week, and the object is clearly stated; namely, 'that there be no gatherings when I come.' Let us read some other translations.

"'And concerning the collection which is for the saints;—as I directed the congregations of Galatia, so also do you. Every first day of the week, let each of you lay something by itself, depositing as he may be prospered, so that when I come collections may not then be made' (1 Cor. 16:1, 2— *Emphatic Diaglott).*

"'But concerning collections…on the first day of the week, let each one of you put by itself, treasuring up, whatsoever he may be prospered with; lest, whensoever I may come, then collections may be in *progress.'—Rotherham."*

"James McKnight renders: 'On the first day of every week, let each of you lay somewhat by itself, according as he may have prospered, putting it into the treasury, that when I come there may be then no collections.'

"The law-teachers argue that this means only that each one should put something in a treasury at home every first day; but the Word is too plain to be thus twisted. The following facts prove their interpretation wrong: Two things were to be done:

first, 'lay somewhat by itself'; second, 'putting it into the treasury,' 'depositing.'

"Now we shall prove that the church in every city kept one general treasury; and there is not the slightest hint of every man's keeping a private treasury at home. The order of the apostle to deposit in the general chest at the weekly meetings every first day we find regularly carried out from that time on through the first centuries.

"Thus says Justin in the middle of the second century, under the head of *'The weekly worship of the Christians':* 'And on the day called Sunday, all who live in cities or in the country, gather together to one place, and the memoirs of the apostles or the writings of the prophets are read as long as time permits. And they who are well-to-do, and willing, give what each thinks fit and what is collected is deposited with the president, who succors the orphans and widows, and those in want.' Here is the practice of the very same thing recorded in 1 Cor. 16: 1, 2.

"Says the writer of *Ancient Christianity Exemplified,* page 73, 'The custom in these primitive times seems to have been for everyone, on the Lord's Day, at the close of public worship, to bring to the notice of the assembly the case of the poor, the aged, the widow, or the orphan of whose necessities he has any knowledge; and forthwith provision was made for such from the public fund created by their weekly contributions.'

"Tertullian, at the close of the second century, says, 'What is collected in the public chest is no dishonorable sum, as if it belonged to a purchased religion. Every one makes a small contribution *on a certain day* or when he chooses; provided only he is willing and able, for no one is compelled, all is voluntary.' He further says that upon this general fund was drawn to feed the poor, etc.

"Many other ancient writers speak of this collection on the first day for the needy. This fund was kept in the church, and only at the time of assembling together were the voluntary collections made by which it was kept up.

"What reason or object could there be in requiring everyone

to deposit something at home every first day? Why single out that day? Would not on any other day do as well? Would it not be better to leave the day optional, so they could make the deposit whenever most able to give? Nay, that day was pointed out as the time to give, because the treasury-chest was kept in the place of public meeting, and being assembled, they had an opportunity to deposit what they had separated for that purpose. Remember the subject is 'concerning collections.' But nothing of that kind could occur if there were no assembly on that day. Every man putting something away at home is no collection at all. The Adventist theory is directly opposite to the apostolic order. It would require, the first thing after the apostle's arrival, that collections be made of all the home deposits. But the system enjoined by the apostle was to avoid that very thing—'that there be no gatherings when I come.' 'So that when I come collections may not then be made.'—*Emphatic Diaglott.* The collections were to be made on the first day of the week 'in order that when I come collections must not first of all be taken.'—*German*

"Had this modern theory been in Paul's mind, he would naturally have explained the object of laying their benefactions in store at home in language something like this: 'That when I come collections of the same may, for the first thing, take place.' But no, the whole matter of collections was to be accomplished before his arrival—'lest whensoever I come, then collections may be in progress.' He speaks of only one thing in reference to the matter to be attended to after his arrival at Corinth. 'But whensoever I may arrive, whomsoever ye may approve, the same will I send to bear away your favor unto Jerusalem.'— Rotherham (vs. 3).

"These few instances of the church's assembling on the first day, with this apostolic law pointing out a duty to be performed upon *'every first day,'* which could be done only in public meeting, are sufficient to convince any humble, honest mind of the Lord's Day, especially since the inspired record furnishes not one instance of the church's meeting on any other *day.*"—*The Sabbath.*

Third. The day of the resurrection, on which the Christian church regularly met for divine worship, is termed in Scripture "the Lord's Day" (Rev. 1:10).

Fourth. The uniform testimony of the early Christian writers that lived immediately after the death of the apostles and during the first centuries of the Christian era is that the church universally regarded Sunday as a memorial day of the resurrection, and held their weekly meetings on that day, calling it "the Lord's Day."

Fifth. The first day of the week is preeminently the great memorial day of the gospel because of what occurred on it. In the new dispensation, under the gospel, what is there in the events of the seventh day to inspire the Christian or to make it a memorial day? Nothing. Jesus was in the grave.

1.   "On Sunday Jesus rose from the dead (Mark 16:9).

2.   "On this day he first appeared to his disciples.

3.   "On this day he met them at different places and repeatedly (Mark 16:9-11; Matt. 28:8-10; Luke 24:34; Mark 16:12, 13; John 20:19-23).

4.   "On this day Jesus blessed them (John 20:19)."

5.   "Here he first commissioned them to preach the gospel to all the world (John 20:21; with Mark 16:9-15).

6.   "Here he gave the apostles authority to legislate for and guide the church (John 20:23).

7.   "Peter says God 'hath begotten us again unto a lively hope by the resurrection of Jesus Christ from the dead' (1 Pet. 1:3).

8.   "Here this day became the day of joy and rejoicing to the disciples. 'Then were the disciples glad When they saw the Lord' (John 20:20). 'While they yet believed not for joy' (Luke 24:41).

9.   "On that day the gospel of a risen Christ was first preached, saying: 'The Lord is risen indeed' (Luke 24:34).

10. "On that Sunday Jesus himself set the example of preaching the gospel of his resurrection by explaining all the

scriptures on that subject and by opening the minds of the disciples to understand it (Luke 24:27, 45)."

11. On that day the early church were assembled in meeting, and Jesus met with them, and said, "Peace be unto you" (Luke 24:33-36).

12. On Sunday the Holy Ghost was poured out upon the infant church, and it was fully organized and set in working order (Acts 2).

13. On that day three thousand souls were added to the number of believers—"a nation was born in one day."

14. Finally, on this day the purchase of our redemption was completed.

"With all these thrilling events of gospel facts crowded into that one resurrection day, making it memorable above all days in the history of the world, how could it but become the great day in the memory of the church? The facts of that one day became the theme of the church ever since. The great battle between the apostles and the unbelieving Jews was concerning the events of that day; did Jesus rise, or did he not? The Jews gave 'large money' to disprove it (Matt. 28:12), while the apostles built the church and staked their lives upon it. Thus in God's own providence, the Jewish Sabbath was thrown into the shade, while all the hopes and thoughts and arguments and songs of the new church were necessarily turned to another day, the resurrection day.

"Memorial day, one that should stir the heart of every Christian and move sinners to repentance, as indeed it has done every week from that day on. 'The Lord's Day,' how appropriate the title for that grand day on which our Lord triumphed over all and laid deep and secure the foundation of the Christian church! Most appropriately, then, has it become the one memorial day of the gospel, the day of gladness and rejoicing."—*Seventh-day Adventism Renounced.*

Sixth. The testimony of lexicons, cyclopedias, and commentaries is uniform in applying the Lord's Day to Sunday. "The Lord's Day. The first day of the week."— *Dr. Clarke* (on

Rev. 1:10).

"The Lord's Day...the first day of the week." —*Eclectic Commentary* (on Rev. 1:10).

"Lord's Day, namely, the first day of the week."— *Burkett's Notes* (on the N. T.)

"The Lord's Day. The first day of the week, commemorating the Lord's resurrection." — *Family Bible* (Notes on Rev. 1:10).

"On the Lord's Day, which can be meant of no other than the day on which the Lord Jesus arose from the dead, even the first day of the week."—*Scott* (on Rev. 1:10).

Dr. Barnes testifies the same.

"Sunday, the first day of the week;...the Lord's *Day.*"— *Webster.*

"Lord's Day. The first day of the week, or Sunday, of every age of the church."—Smith's *Dictionary of the Bible.*

"It is called the Lord's Day."—*Buck's Theological Dictionary.*

"Lord's day, a name for the first day of the week, derived from Rev. 1 :10."—*Johnson's New Universal Cyclopedia.*

The same will be found in Greenfield's, Robison's, Liddel & Scott's, Parkhurst's, Bagster's, and all other lexicons. There is reason why all these learned men who have thoroughly investigated the matter agree that Sunday is the Lord's Day. The testimony of truth and that of the early church is overwhelming on this point.

Many other sound reasons could be given why Christians keep the Lord's Day as a memorial day, but we deem the six foregoing reasons a sufficient apology for our regard for the resurrection day.

The Lord's Day Prefigured in the Old Testament

The great memorial day of the gospel seems to have been clearly prefigured in the law of shadows.

1. The Feast of Harvest. "Speak unto the children of Israel, and say unto them, 'When ye be come into the land which

I give unto you, and shall reap the harvest thereof, then ye shall bring a sheaf of the first-fruits of your harvest unto the priest: and he shall wave the sheaf before the Lord, to be accepted for you: *on the morrow after the Sabbath* the priest shall wave it" (Lev. 23:10, 11).

This took place "on the morrow after the Sabbath." This was the eighth day, or the first day of the week. The sheaf that the priest waved before the Lord was of the "first-fruits of the harvest." What did it typify? Paul gives the answer: "But now is Christ risen from the dead, and become the first-fruits of them that slept" (1 Cor. 15:20). That sheaf clearly pointed to the resurrection of Christ. True to the shadow, Christ rose on the first day of the week. So the *eighth day* on which the wave-offering was made, was a part of the shadow as much as the offering. As certain as the sheaf pointed to the resurrection of Christ, so certain did the eighth day on which it took place point to the day on which he arose—the Lord's Day. That sheaf was a sample of the entire crop, so Christ's resurrection is a sample and proof of the future resurrection of all the redeemed (see 1 Corinthians 15).

2.   The Feast of Pentecost. "And ye shall count unto you from the morrow after the Sabbath, from the day that ye brought the sheaf of the wave-offering; seven Sabbaths shall be complete: even unto the morrow after the seventh Sabbath shall ye number fifty days; and ye shall offer a new meat-offering unto the Lord. And ye shall offer with the bread seven lambs without blemish of the first year, and one young bullock, and two rams: they shall be for a burnt offering unto the Lord, with their meat-offering, and their drink-offerings, even an offering made by fire, of sweet savor unto the Lord" (Lev. 23:15, 16, 18).

This offering "made by fire" pointed to the baptism of "the Holy Ghost and fire" received on Pentecost. The Feast of Pentecost was on the *"morrow after the seventh Sabbath,"* or fifty days from the wave-offering. "Pentecost" means fifty. How wonderful this shadow! The sheaf was waved before the Lord on the *first day of the week.* It pointed to Christ's resurrection, which took place on the same day. Just seven weeks later came the Feast of Pentecost, an offering by fire. That fell also on the day "after the Sabbath." Just seven weeks after Christ's resurrection the Holy Spirit fire fell on one hundred and twenty, and the church of God was organized. Both took place on the first day of the week.

In the law of shadows we read: "And ye shall proclaim on the selfsame day, that it may be a holy convocation unto you" (Lev. 23:21). "Convocation" means assembly. "On the *first day* shall be an holy convocation....On the eighth day shall be an holy convocation unto you; and ye shall offer an offering made by fire unto the Lord: it is a solemn assembly" (vss. 35, 36). "On the eighth day ye shall have a solemn assembly" (Num. 29:35). "On the eighth day they made a solemn assembly" (2 Chron. 7:9). "On the eighth day was a solemn assembly" (Neh. 8:18). All this was a shadow. Notice that the eighth day, or first day of the week, stood out in great prominence.

The two feasts held on this day pointed to the two great triumphant events in the plan of redemption; viz., the resurrection of Christ and the outpouring of the Holy Spirit. In the type, the eighth day was a day of assembly, a day when sacrifice by fire was offered to the Lord. This foreshadowed the great memorial day of the gospel—the Lord's Day. From the day on which Christ rose from the dead, the eighth day has been a day of assembling, a day of holy convocation for the church of God, a day when sacrifices of praise and thanksgiving by the Holy Spirit's fire have been given to God.

How The Lord's Day Should Be Observed

Since the rigorous, severe Sabbatical character of the Jewish Sabbath does not belong to the memorial day of the gospel, some have gone to the opposite extreme, and cast aside all regard for the day, and have taken liberty to do all kinds of temporal work and business. This is both unwise and contrary to the Scriptural teaching. Why is the resurrection day termed "the Lord's day" if no more regard is to be given to it than to the other days of the week? This day should be given to the Lord. Some may say we give every day to the Lord by living a godly life. This is true in the sense that we must serve God in holiness all our days. But there is another sense in which we can set apart one day of the week for the Lord. We can dispense with our temporal affairs and devote this day to spiritual worship, joyfulness, and labor for the salvation of the lost. This is exactly what the primitive church did. All ordinances of God are established either by positive precept or by clear example. We have the sacredness of the resurrection day handed down to us by the example of the primitive church.

From the great day of Pentecost until now this has been a day of gospel preaching, a day of salvation work. It has always been my busiest day. During the thirty years of my ministry it has never been a day of rest and recreation. But it is a day of spiritual labor. More souls have been won to Christ on this day than on all the other days of the week put together. I am fully convinced that as far as possible all secular work should be put aside, and this memorial Lord's Day should be spent in spiritual work for God. The church of God should make it the day of mighty effort in spreading the saving truth and redeeming the lost.

The Pope and the Sabbath

By constantly crying in the ears of the people: "Sunday is a heathen day; and all who observe it keep 'the venerable day of the sun'" "The bishop of Rome is authority for Sunday observance"; "Constantine changed the Sabbath"; "The observance of the first day of the week began with the pope of Rome," etc., etc., Adventists frighten a few ignorant souls into this belief; and the result is, they cease to observe the great memorial day of the gospel, and go back under the "yoke of bondage." This man of straw is one of the most effectual means in the hands of Sabbatarians. But the whole is wrong from the ground up. Not a word of truth is there in any of the assertions quoted. The facts of history utterly refute them. Let us examine.

The heathens never kept Sunday, as Adventists affirm. I

quote from Canright:

'Such statements are utterly false. Each day of the week was named after some god, and, in a certain sense, was devoted to the worship of that god, as Monday to the moon, Saturday to Saturn, Sunday to the sun, etc. But did they cease work on these days? No; if they had they would have kept every day in the week. Did they observe Sunday by ceasing to work? No indeed. No such thing was taught or practiced by the Romans. They had no weekly rest-day.

'Prof. A. Rauschinbusch, of Rochester Theological Seminary, quotes Lotz thus: "It is a vain thing to attempt to prove that the Greeks and Romans had anything resembling the Sabbath. Such opinion is refuted even by this, that the Roman writers ridicule the Sabbath as something peculiar to the Jews.' In proof he cites many passages from the Roman poets, and one from Tacitus. Seneca also condemned the Sabbath observance of the Jews as a waste if time by which a seventh part of life was lost."—*Saturday or Sunday?* (page 83). "No special religious celebration of any one day of the week can be pointed out in any one of the pagan religions.—"Herzog *(Art. "Sabbath.")* The pagans never kept Sunday. So much for that. *Saturday was sacred to Saturn* as Sunday was to the sun.' So if Christians keep a heathen day, Adventists also do.

Next we inquire, Did Constantine change the Sabbath? Adventist literature and teachings say, "Yes." History and facts say, "No." Notice the Adventists' dilemma. One time they cry, "Constantine changed the Sabbath," and again they say, "It was the pope." Pray how can this be? Constantine's Sunday law was made in A. D. 321, long years before there was a pope recognized as controlling Christendom. Then, their talk about the pope's changing the observance of the day is refuted by their own literature, which teaches that it was Constantine. Now comes the climax. Elder Waggoner, a leading Adventist, finally admits that "it is safe to affirm that there was nothing done in the time of Constantine, either by himself or any other that has the least appearance of changing the Sabbath." —*Replies to Elder*

Canright, (page 150). Amen. Then, from their own admission, we are forced to conclude that they know better themselves when they try to scare the people into believing that Constantine or the pope of Rome changed the observance of the day.

The facts are, as proved in preceding chapters, that the Christian church observed the Lord's Day as the great memorial day of the gospel, from the resurrection day on. When Constantine was converted, or became favorable to the Christian religion, he simply issued an edict throughout his empire for people to observe the Christian's day. That is all there is to it. "The first day of the week, which was the ordinary and stated time for the public assemblies of the Christians, was, in consequence of a peculiar law enacted by Constantine, observed with greater solemnity than it had formerly been."—*Mosheim* (Part II, chap. 4. sec. 5). The united testimony of the early Christian writers as seen in a preceding chapter, was that they all held Sunday as a sacred and memorial day, and this long before Constantine's time.

The following quotation is from *The Sabbath.* After quoting Mrs. White, who says in her book *Great Controversy* that the observance of days was changed by Constantine and the bishop of Rome, the writer, D. S. Warner, says:

"Look at the impudence of this prophetess! The apostle John called the resurrection day 'the Lord's day' in A. D. 96. She says that title was conferred upon it by the bishop of Rome in the fourth century. She speaks of the 'false' and the 'true,' calling the first day of the week the false and the seventh day the true. But eighteen hundred years before she was born, Justin Martyr wrote under the same head, and denounced the Jewish Sabbath as the false, and declared the first day the true Lord's day. He wrote in the virgin purity of Christianity; she writes under the thick fogs of Babel confusion. He wrote as the Apostle did who pronounced the curse of God upon the false teachers who troubled the Galatian church, 'subverting the gospel of Christ' by enjoining the law and its 'days.' She writes largely the doctrine of the Ebionites, one of the first and most abominable heresies.

"She says that in the first centuries the seventh day had been kept by all Christians. And her own word is the only proof she offers. But we have seen that both the Word of God and the early church Fathers teach us that only persons who were weak and ignorant of the liberties of the sons of God thought it necessary to observe the law respecting meats and the Sabbaths. And Justin told Trypho that the Sabbath of the law belonged only to the Jews, and that it was not proper for Christians to observe it; and by others we are positively told that Saturday was a common work-day in the primitive church of God. This prophetess leaves the impression that Constantine, as a heathen, enjoined the observance of Sunday as a public festival, and after his professed conversion still adhered to it, thus making him the author of that day of worship. So Adventism teaches. But all readers of the New Testament and of early history know better. For two hundred years before Constantine's day, in fact from the resurrection of Christ, the first day was kept by the church of God, as a memorial day, a weekly day of worship. Constantine had nothing to do with the establishment of the Lord's Day in the church. God's institutions need no kingly decrees. But what that emperor did simply related to the day in his empire.

"Should the head of the Chinese empire become specially favorable to the Christian religion, nothing would be more natural than that he would adopt the first day of the week as their national holiday. This is substantially what Constantine did. Yet there is no more reason of truth in ascribing to him the origin of the observance of the Lord's Day than there would be in making the emperor of China father of it, were he to do the same thing in this century. When Constantine called the first day 'the venerable day of the sun,' he had no reference to any idolatrous use of that day. More than a hundred years before, the days of the week had all been named after planets, as follows: the first day after the Sun—Sunday; the next after the moon—Monday; the last after Saturn—Saturday; etc. And these names had passed into common use. Constantine, having been convinced of the truth of the Christian religion, would naturally speak of the preeminence of their day of worship, of which preeminence he had a beautiful illustration of the fact that the sun is the greatest planet of the solar system, and the source of all light. So this constant cry of Adventism that 'Constantine changed the Sabbath,' etc., is false. And no person can inform himself of the historical facts and make the assertion without knowing he is wrong. They dispute the plain scriptures, renounce all early history that exposes their creed, and virtually make their own history to suit their purpose.

"They are now sending out two pamphlets, the first of which is entitled *Rome's Challenge, Why do Protestants Keep Sunday?* the second, *Our Answer.* In the first, Roman authorities are quoted, affirming that they changed the day from the seventh to the first day; that there is no evidence in Scripture or early history in favor of the first-day observance; that it rests only upon Rome's authority to change the laws of God. To this false statement Adventists give consent, and then claim to be persecuted because they do not keep the day Rome made. But God's Word and the writings of the church Fathers rebuke both."

After Waggoner (Adventist) admitted that Constantine did not change the Sabbath, he then attempted to fix the Council of Laodicea, A. D. 364, as the exact place where and time when the pope made the change. Adventists of late accept Waggoner's position. The twenty-ninth canon of that council reads thus: "Christians ought not to Judaize and to rest in the Sabbath, but to work in that day; but preferring the Lord's Day, should rest, if possible, as Christians. Wherefore if they shall be found to Judaize, let them be accursed from Christ." On this Waggoner says, "Now, if anyone can imagine what would be changing the Sabbath, if this is not, I would be extremely happy to learn what it could be." As a thorough refutation of the Adventists' position on this important point, I quote the following facts and able arguments from *Seventh-day Adventism Renuonced:*

"1. If the Sabbath was changed to Sunday by the pope right here, as he affirms, then certainly it was not changed before nor after nor at any other place. So if this fails their whole cause is lost. Let the reader mark the importance of this fact.

"2. He admits what every scholar knows, that till after the time of Constantine the bishop of Rome had no 'authority whatever above the other bishops' and so could not have changed the Sabbath before that time. He says: 'It was Constantine himself that laid the foundation of the papacy.'— *Replies to Elder Canright,* (page 148). Surely the papacy did not exist before its foundation was laid.

"3. He admits, as above, that Constantine did nothing to change the Sabbath.

"4. But we have abundantly proved in preceding pages that all Christians long before this date were unanimous in observing the Lord's Day. This one simple fact proves the utter absurdity of the claim that it was changed at Laodicea, A. D. 364, or by the papacy at any time.

"5. In the year 324, or just forty years before the Council of Laodicea, Eusebius, bishop of Caesarea, Palestine, wrote his celebrated history of Christianity. He had every possible opportunity to know what Christians did throughout the world. He says: 'And all things whatsoever it was the duty to do on the Sabbath, these we have transferred to the Lord's Day as more honorable than the Jewish Sabbath.'—*Quoted in Sabbath Manual* (page 127)

"That is the way the Sabbath and Sunday stood forty years before Laodicea. They did not keep the Sabbath, but did keep the Lord's Day...How much truth, then, can there be in the position that the Sabbath was changed to Sunday by the pope forty years later? Shame on such attempts to pervert the truth. But let us look at the real facts about the Council of Laodicea. Seventh-day Adventists claim two things, viz., that the Sabbath was changed by the Roman church, and that it was done by the authority of the pope. Then they select Laodicea as the place and time. But—

"1. Laodicea is not Rome. It is situated in Asia Minor over one thousand miles east of Rome. It was in Asia, not in Europe. It was an Eastern, not a Western town, an Oriental, not a Latin city.

"2.   It was a Greek, not a Roman city.

"3. The pope of Rome did not attend this Council at Laodicea, A. D. 364. Does Waggoner claim that he did? No, he does not dare to.

"4.   The pope did not attend, nor did he send a legate or a delegate or anyone to represent him. In fact, neither the Roman Catholic Church, nor the pope had anything to do with the council in any way, shape, or manner. It was held without even their knowledge or consent.

"5.   At this early date, A. D. 364, the popes, or rather bishops of Rome, had no authority over other bishops. It was two hundred years later before they were invested with authority over all the churches. Even then their authority was stoutly resisted for centuries in the East where this council was held. See *Bower's History of Popes,* or any church history.

"6.   Liberius was bishop of Rome at the time of this council at Laodicea. He was degraded from his office, banished, and treated with the utmost contempt. Bower says that in order to end his exile, Liberius 'wrote in a most submissive and cringing style to the eastern Bishops.'—*History of the Popes* (vol. 1, p. 64). And this was the pope who changed the Sabbath at a council of these same Eastern bishops, one thousand miles away, which he never attended!

"7.   The council of Laodicea was only a local council, a small, unimportant affair, and not a general council at all....The general councils are: 1. That at Nice, A. D. 325. 2. That at Constantinople, A. D. 381. 3. That at Ephesus, A. D. 431, etc. See the list in *Johnson's Cyclopedia,* or any history. Bower in his extensive work, the *History of the Popes,* gives an account of all the general councils, the important local councils, and all with which Rome or the popes had to do, but does not even mention this one at Laodicea....'This council is not even mentioned by Mosheim, Milner, Ruter, Reeves, Socrates, Sozomen, nor by four other historians on my table.' *McClintock and Strong's Cyclopedia* says: 'Thirty-two bishops were present from different provinces in Asia.' All bishops of the Eastern church, *not one from the Roman church!* And yet this was the time and place when and where the Roman church and the pope changed the Sabbath.

"8. Now think of it: this little local council of thirty-two bishops revolutionizes the whole world on the keeping of the Sabbath!

"9. The fact is that this council simply regulated in this locality an already long-established institution, the Lord's Day, just the same as council after council did afterwards....The Lord's Day had been kept by the church hundreds of years before the council of Laodicea mentioned it.

"10. The church of Laodicea where this council was held was raised up by Paul himself....It was one of the seven churches to which John wrote (Rev. 3:14). Hence it is certain that it was well instructed and grounded in the doctrines of the apostles. Between Paul and this council, that is, A. D. 270, Anatolius was bishop of Laodicea. He wrote: "Our regard for the Lord's resurrection, which took place on the Lord's Day, will lead us to celebrate it on the same principle' (Canon 16). Here we have that church keeping Sunday one hundred years before this council.

"11. Finally, if the Council of Laodicea changed the Sabbath, as Adventists say, then it was changed by the Greek church instead of the Roman church; changed by the Eastern churches over which Rome had no authority; changed before the papacy was established, before the pope had an authority over the East, by a small local council which neither the pope nor any of his servants attended. The absurdity of this claim is manifest without further argument."

Sunday-Keeping Is Not the Mark of the Beast

"Sunday-keeping must be the mark of the beast."—*The Marvel of Nations,* by U. Smith (page 183).

"The seal of God is his holy *Sabbath.*"—*Thoughts on Revelation* (page 452).

These give the Seventh-day Adventist doctrine in its full force. All, then, who keep the Jewish Sabbath are sealed for eternal bliss. This would include the Pharisees, and all Jews, Seventh-day Baptists, and Seventh-day Adventists. The teeming millions of earth that do not keep the seventh day are not sealed; cannot be. If the Sabbath is the seal of God, then all who disregard it, and keep the Lord's Day, are not sealed. What, then, is their condition? Smith answers "Sunday-keeping must be the mark of the beast." All who keep Sunday, therefore, are of necessity beast-worshipers. Listen. "Sunday-keeping is an institution of the first beast, and all who submit to obey this institution emphatically worship the first beast and receive his mark, 'the mark of the beast.'...Those who worship the beast and his image *by observing the first day* are certainly *idolaters.*"—*Advent Review Extra* (August, 1850, pages 10, 11). Uriah Smith says that those who keep the first day are "thereby marked" *(The Marvel of Nations,* pages 174, 175). The Revelator says that all who worship the beast and receive his mark will be cast into eternal torment (Rev. 14:9-11). So, to sum up the whole, all who keep the Sabbath are "sealed" for eternal glory, while all who observe the Lord's Day are "beast-worshipers," "idolaters," "marked," and doomed to "eternal torment."

Surely such absurdity should awaken even those who have been ensnared into that dark yoke of legal bondage. Luther, Wesley, Huss, Bunyan, Milton, Baxter, and all the other great and good men down through the ages who effected mighty reformations in the earth and were powers in the hands of God, all rejected the seventh day and were Sunday-keepers. But according to the foregoing quotations from the Adventist literature, they were all "marked by the beast" and were "idolaters." But the Adventists themselves admit that these very men were Christians. This admission overthrows their position that Sunday-keeping is the mark of the beast. I again quote from *Adventism Renounced:*

"Mrs. White says of him [Luther]: 'Zealous, ardent, and devoted, knowing no fear but the fear of God, and acknowledging no foundation for religious faith but the holy Scriptures,' etc. 'Angels of heaven were by his side, and rays of light from the throne of God revealed the treasures of truth to his understanding.'—*Great Controversy* (pages 94, 97). Good. Now hear Luther. Carlstadt, a zealous and learned Sabbatarian, laid his arguments for the seventh day before Luther, who examined them. Here is Luther's decision in his own words: 'Indeed, if Carlstadt were to write further about the Sabbath, Sunday would have to give way, and the Sabbath—that is to say, Saturday— must be kept holy; he would truly make us Jews in all things, and we should come to be circumcised; for that is true and cannot be denied, that he who deems it necessary to keep one law of Moses, and keeps it as the law of Moses, must deem all necessary, and keep them all.' —*History Sabbath* (page 457)."

Luther heard the teaching on Sabbath observance; but he, like true Christians today, rejected it. Mrs. White admits that "angels and light from God's throne" revealed the truth to Luther. Amen. Then, Luther was clear in his observance of the Lord's Day and his rejection of the Jewish Sabbath.

"Hear Mrs. White on John Bunyan: 'John Bunyan breathed the very atmosphere of heaven' (*Great Controversy*, page 174). Well, now hear Bunyan: 'As for the seventh-day Sabbath, that, as we see, is gone to its grave with the signs and shadows of the Old Testament; yea, and it has such a dash left upon it by apostolic authority, that it is enough to make a Christian fly from it forever (2 Corinthians 3)'—*Complete Works* (page 915)." So Bunyan, who breathed "the atmosphere of heaven," rejected and opposed the observance of the Jewish Sabbath.

Thank God for these admissions from the great prophetess of Adventism. So we today, with Luther, Wesley, Baxter, and Bunyan, reject the Jewish Sabbath, and keep the great memorial day of the gospel; and while doing so *breathe the atmosphere of heaven. Hallelujah!*

Instead of Sabbath-keeping being the seal of God, the Bible plainly states that the seal is the Holy Spirit. 'Who hath also sealed us, and given the earnest of the Spirit in our hearts" (2

Cor. 1:22). "In whom ye also trusted, after that ye heard the word of truth, the gospel of your salvation: in whom also after that ye believed, ye were sealed with that Holy Spirit of promise" (Eph. 1:13). "And grieve not the Holy Spirit of God, whereby ye are sealed unto the day of redemption" (Eph. 4:30).

Nowhere does the Bible state that the observance of the Lord's Day is the mark of the beast. To assert such a thing is bare assumption, without one text of proof. It is false for the following reasons:

1.   The first day of the week was the day upon which the early Christians held their meetings and met for divine worship. This we have conclusively proved.

2.   The united testimony of the early Christian writers who wrote but a few years after the death of the apostles, and during the first few centuries of the Christian era, testify that the church in their time regarded the resurrection day as the great memorial day of the gospel, and termed it the Lord's Day. This was long before the beast arose.

3.   The Catholic sect did not change the observance of days from the seventh to the first. This we have abundantly proved.

4.   The Adventists quote a few old Catholic catechisms as their only proof that the beast changed the Sabbath; and in this they misrepresent the Catholic teaching, as any scholar knows. So whatever the mark of the beast in the forehead and right hand may signify, it cannot be the observance of the great memorial day of the gospel.

THE END

Other Books Published by Life Assurance Ministries

- *Sabbath in Crisis*, by Dale Ratzlaff, 351 pages, $14.95. This is a thorough, yet easy to read, biblical study on the gospel, the Sabbath and the old and new covenants.

  "Your book, *Sabbath in Crisis,* has been instrumental in my transition from my legalistic belief and practice...to my transformed newness of life in my relationship with my Savior, Jesus Christ. No experience has been as profound or as important in my life...I also have used your book as a basis for Bible studies in our Christian fellowship and have literally seen the miracle of awareness come upon believers as the veil was lifted by Jesus Christ"—Pastor David Davidson, Mountain Home, Arkansas

- *The Cultic Doctrine of Seventh-day Adventists—An Evangelical Resource, An Appeal to SDA Leadership*, by Dale Ratzlaff, 388 pages, $14.95

  "Ratzlaff's writing clearly possesses a spirit of meekness; it is nevertheless a *tour de force.* Patiently pursuing his subject, he lays out the evidence supporting an irresistible conclusion—Ellen White was not a true prophet or messenger from God, and the Seventh-day Adventist Church is not what it claims to be, the only true "remnant church." If Adventist leadership will heed his plea, then perhaps this church is salvageable. If not, then it is time for evangelicals everywhere to say to the Christians within Adventism, with neither malice nor exultation, but with one united and very earnest voice, "Babylon is fallen! Come out of her my people!" —Timothy Oliver, Editor, Researcher at Watchman Fellowship

- *The Truth About Seventh-day Adventist "Truth"*, by Dale Ratzlaff, 44 pages, $3.95.

  "Seventh-day Adventist teachings are rapidly spreading around the world. For decades there has been a need for a clear and concise biblical examination of the fundamental teachings of this church. This ready reference on Adventism compares biblical Christianity with contemporary Adventism and quickly gives the reader an understanding of the major issues and answers. *The Truth About Seventh-day Adventist "Truth"* is a ministry tool that will equip many to meet the questions of those interested in Adventism as well as share the Gospel with the searching thousands within the Seventh-day Adventist church.—J. Mark Martin, Senior Pastor, Calvary Community Church, Phoenix, Arizona.

- *A Theologian's Journey from Seventh-day Adventism to Mainstream Christianity*, by Jerry Gladson, Ph.D., Senior Minister at First Christian Church (Disciples of Christ), Marietta, Georgia, 383 pages, $17.95.

  "Dr. Gladson was a SDA theologian, professor and pastor serving an important role at the central core of Adventist scholarship for many years. Drawing from his meticulously kept journals, Dr. Gladson describes events at the center of the recent crisis in Adventism. He has done something few other scholars have been able to do. He has combined careful, detailed research with a gripping, narrative style of writing. The reader is forced to crawl under the skin of Dr. Gladson, see through his eyes and feel the trauma of having to choose between career and conscience. One cannot put the book down until finished. This book uncovers the hidden, toxic core of Adventism" —Dale Ratzlaff

- ***White Washed, Uncovering the Myths of Ellen G. White,*** by Sydney Cleveland, 233 pages, $12.95.

  White Washed is a comprehensive look at Ellen White's prophecies, practices and publications. Sydney Cleveland examines her claims of inspiration, her dreams and visions, the doctrines she endorsed her personal practices that opposed her teachings and the effect of her claims on the Adventist Church. This is a well-documented overview of the little-known reality about Ellen White and her long service to the Adventist church. Sydney Cleveland was an Adventist pastor for 11 years. During an extensive study of Ellen G. White's writings, he discovered that she contradicted the Holy Bible, gave many false prophecies, and didn't even follow her own teachings.

- **Other Materials**: Life Assurance Ministries Publications carries an inventory of other materials including books, videos and cassette tapes designed to minister to former or inquiring Seventh-day Adventists, sabbatarians and concerned Evangelicals. For contact information, please see the first pages of this book.